From Fat, Black, and Unlovable to

Beautiful
POWERFUL
LOVE

a journey of intergenerational healing and transformation

Barbara C. Pamplin

Foreword by
Chief Oluwo Obafemi Ifayemi Epega

DIGITAL ADIMU
TRANSFORMATIONAL CONTENT

Digital Adimu, LLC
1400 112the Ave SE
Suite 100
Bellevue, 98004
Published in 2019
Published in the United States

ISBN 978-1-7336404-0-4 Print edition
ISBN 978-1-7336404-1-1 e-Book edition
ISBN 978-1-7336404-2-8 Audiobook edition

FOR MAMA AND ALL MY ANCESTRAL MOTHERS

QUESSIE MAXINE (INGRAM) WILLIAMS
SUNRISE OCTOBER 23, 1937 - SUNSET JULY 15, 2006

Children, I come back today
To tell you a story of the long dark way
That I had to climb, that I had to know
In order that the race might live and grow.

Langston Hughes, *The Negro Mother*

Table of Contents

FOREWORD

Since the beginning of time, people have been born and they have transitioned. Mankind has always pondered what happens during this process of coming and going. Since no one has ever come back to tell us, we have relied on dreams, epiphanies, and déjà vu experiences to understand the cycle of life and death. Stories about crossing over were made into mythology as ways to understand death and transition, death and rebirth, death and resurrection. Despite these myths, no human has ever died and later seen alive in the same physical form. Even though many spiritual traditions across the globe believe in the concept of reincarnation, most people do not think it to be possible. However, the first law of thermodynamics tells us that energy doesn't die, it simply takes on a different form. We also understand the human spirit as energy that lives within the body and within the breath. In Ifa we call the breath "emi," which also means the spirit or soul that works with the Ori (your higher consciousness). Emi can also be interpreted as an individual's ancestor spirit in heaven, the part of them that is an ancestor returned. Energy or spirit, including the ancestor spirit, enters the body of the baby through the breath and leaves the full-grown adult with their last breath at death.

In Ifa practicing communities throughout West Africa, a ceremony called an "essentaye" is held for new babies in the family. The word essentaye means "feet touch the earth" and for a Western comparison, the ceremony can be likened to a christening. At three days old, the baby's purpose and path of destiny is determined by elders in the community, along with the identity and lineage of the ancestor that has returned as the new baby. While performing this ceremony, the community honors the ancestors by acknowledging their return as a new person to do new things but who may share characteristics with the ancestor. This concept of birth and rebirth is the circle of life and is the journey which started before the baby and continues with and after the baby's life.

Ancestor reverence was born out of the idea of honoring those that came before us and enabled our physical existence on earth. We honor them because we believe in the circle of life. We realize that our clearest understanding of spirit is through our blood relatives that have transitioned and exist in the spirit realm. As individuals in the Diaspora who descended from enslaved ancestors, we may find ourselves having thoughts, memories, or emotions that are intense beyond our understanding. For example, you may find that closed spaces, traveling by boat, or sitting under a tree, triggers feelings of panic. This can be explained by corporeal Akashic records, the collective memories of our ancestors held within our bodies. When these memories are triggered, our ancestors can help us to understand the meaning in an effort to live free of "post traumatic slave syndrome." Ancestral reverence is key to our healing.

Thus, as part of our spiritual practice, we seek our ancestors' guidance through prayer and meditation to help us through difficulties of life. Our ancestors are always with us, urging us to make right decisions when we find ourselves at the crossroads. Sister Barbara was approaching a crossroads in her life when she came to me for a reading in 2016. Throughout the reading, her ancestors showed strong support and encouraged her to write in order to realize her healing. This book is the product of Barbara's openness and obedience to her ancestors' guidance. In it she expresses her pain and the collective pain of her ancestors held in her heart. By sharing her story with others, she has taken steps to craft her own narrative and that of those that came before her. Barbara empowers her readers by laying out her healing process and transformation through her struggles. The words that flowed through her onto these pages have served to not only uplift her, but to uplift others as well. By reading her story, we witness the power of ancestral reverence and the transformation of osobo into ire.

Ase. Ase. Ase O!
Chief Oluwo Obafemi Ifayemi Epega
Founder and President of OIDSI
December 2018

Obafemi Institute for the Divine & Universal Study of Ifa
(OIDSI)
P.O. Box 2188, Missouri City, TX 77459
www.obafemi.org

PREFACE

The spiral of 2020

Healing of any type, be it physical, mental, emotional, or spiritual, is a process. A famous fictional character described his personality as an onion in that he had layers. Similarly, healing is layered and multidimensional as well. Just when you think you have done the work, learned the lessons, and transformed your life, you are faced with deeper wounds to heal, greater truths to realize, and more changes to make. In fact, healing is literally a process that manifests as a spiral.

By the time I completed writing this book in December 2018 and when I published it in March 2019, my life was fundamentally different than it was before. In my mind, my healing was well on its way and the life changes I needed to make were nearly complete. Little did I know it was all just beginning.

I wrote this preface in the fall of 2020, at a point in time when the entire planet and all of humanity has been shifting, releasing, and recalibrating for nearly a year. I look back at the major changes that occurred in own my life since 2017 and I can definitively see the spiral at work. Since then, I have experienced the urging of my Ancestors to continue my healing journey. I was called to see and accept deeper truths, even when it was uncomfortable. Then, armed with the confidence that comes with increments of healing and the clear vision that comes with realizing greater truths, I continued to do more to align myself with the resonance of who I am here to be. We are all responsible for manifesting the life we desire and to reclaim our birthright of success and happiness. I could hope, wish, and pray for the peace, love, and joy I wanted but I also had to identify and address the things that brought disruption and discord into my life. Not only did I need to dissolve personal attachments to toxic thoughts, beliefs, and behaviors, but interpersonal cords needed to be healed as well. I had to initiate the necessary death and transmutation of toxic circumstances so that I could align with the energy of my highest self.

When I reread this book, I see my journey shared as my truth at the time that I wrote it. It all holds true but looking back with the insight I have now after continuing to do The Work, I see that there are even greater truths to be shared with my readers. I thought about writing a new updated edition of this book. But my ancestors vehemently said no. This next level of healing, this next level of The Work is to be shared with the world in a new book to come. They explained that my testimonies need to exist as points in time to be authentic and true. This book, together with future works, will provide context through which Black women and femmes can individually and collectively experience the spiral for themselves. I honor my ancestors' guidance and I am obedient - with only the addition of this preface and small corrective edits, this work stands as it was written in 2018.

The purpose of this preface to help my readers understand that more internal work is always required. More sacrifice is always required. More cutting and dissolution of cords is always required. More courage and alignment to your higher self is always required. Greater truths are always seeking your revelation. A deeper, more expansive love of and for you is always present, awaiting your acceptance.

In the meantime, embrace the fact that you are loved, loving, and lovable!

Thank you for all The Work you do on your spiral of healing!

♥ Love & light,
Barbara C. Pamplin (Ohuninifa)
Author, Speaker, Coach, and Founder
BeautifulPowerfulLove.com

INTRODUCTION

The Work I am Here to Do

I don't remember the first two times I died. I have images in my mind, reconstructed from other people's stories and my hospital records, but I don't think what I see is *my* memory. I see a mind movie of the facts as they occurred, but it's devoid of emotion which lets me know it's a re-creation. The doctors have explained that anesthesia can have that effect on the mind, sparring us from traumatic memories.

The first time I died was on November 8th, 2017 at 7:52pm.

I had already been in the Critical Care Unit of Overlake Hospital in Bellevue, Washington for twenty days following an emergency open-heart surgery to repair my aorta. The aorta is the large main artery through which blood pumps out of your heart to every organ and cell in your body. I had an aortic dissection, an acute disorder in which the inner lining of the aortic wall suddenly tears and separates from the middle layer of the aortic wall. There are two types of aorta dissections and I had the type that required an immediate ten-hour open-heart surgery to save my life. I would later learn that it was years of uncontrolled high blood pressure that enlarged my heart and weakened my blood vessels, creating the conditions for the dissection to occur. About 20% of people who have an aortic dissection die before they reach the hospital. Given the many complications that can happen before, during, and after surgery if the patient makes it to the hospital, Type A aortic dissection has a 99% fatality rate (Farber, Ahmad 2019). When the dissection occurred, my brain and kidneys were denied their full supply of blood and oxygen. Even though I survived the surgery to replace part of my aorta with a synthetic material called Dacron, the doctors warned my husband that I may have mental or physical disabilities due to the damage my body sustained. I was in kidney failure after the surgery and required daily dialysis. However, my mental functions were slowly returning, and I was recovering and regaining strength.

I was just a few days from being discharged and was able to walk around the Critical Care Unit. Based on recounts from my husband, doctors, and nurses, I returned to my room the evening of November 8th, 2017 after taking a short walk to the waiting room. I was wearing my son's Santa hat while on a three-way call with my husband and our friend in New York. Shortly after going into the bathroom, (yes, I intended to potty while talking on the phone), my husband said I stopped talking in mid-sentence and all he heard was the cracking sound of my phone hitting the floor. They both started shouting my name with no response. Soon they heard the nurses shouting, "Oh my god, did she break her neck…where is all the blood coming from," and "Code Blue!"

That night, as I chatted on the phone in the bathroom, my heart had suddenly stopped beating. My body collapsed towards the wall closest to the toilet and the weight of my body sliding down pulled the string to signal the nurses that I needed assistance. That was how they found me so quickly and alerted the staff that a "Code Blue" was in progress, meaning a patient was in fatal distress. When my body hit the floor, I severely bit my tongue creating deep gouges that spilled my blood on to the tile. The doctor and nurses were still trying to resuscitate me when my husband made it to the hospital and up to my room. According to my hospital chart, it took twenty-three minutes of manual CPR for my heart to start beating again.

The second time I died was just eight days later November 16th, 2017 at 3:28am.

I had survived and recovered miraculously after the nurses found me on the bathroom floor. Because I flatlined, I had to start over with occupational therapy to relearn how to function while protecting my healing sternum which was further compromised by the necessary manual CPR. I was also working with physical therapists to regain my strength for walking and with the nurses to exercise my collapsed lungs. I was doing well and was, again, just days from discharge. During one of the many and required reviews of my vital signs, my nurse noticed I looked a bit off, even for the middle of the night. According to my hospital records, he asked me if I was ok to which I replied, "I feel terrible." Then my body went stiff and I fell back in my bed, my heart no longer beating, my lungs no longer breathing. My nurse signaled a "Code Blue" and the cavalry came in to save me. They called my husband immediately and, again, he was there by my side as they worked to resuscitate me. This time I was gone for thirty-one minutes. Once I returned to my body with a heartbeat, I was stabilized and intubated. Later that evening I was back in the operating room undergoing a second open-heart surgery. This surgery was to remove a blood clot from one of my ventricles and to check for anything that might have caused my heart to cease beating. They couldn't find anything other than the blood clot that needed repair and couldn't find a clear explanation for why this happened again. When I woke up, I had no idea what had happened. The time between my first and second "Code Blue" was so close that my medicated brain was not clear enough to comprehend that I died once let alone, twice and had a second surgery. It seemed as if I just went to sleep and woke up the next day, not ten days, two deaths, and one more surgery later. Opening my chest for a second time, plus enduring manual CPR twice was a lot for a body to take. Once I was stable, the doctors explained that I had the second surgery and showed me chest x-rays which reflected how they stabilized my sternum with titanium plates. I remember hospital staff and volunteers stopping by to say hello and tell me they were glad I was still with the living. Many people were involved with my care and gave me emotional support and encouragement. It became a regular occurrence to hear "You are a miracle child," and "You are here for a reason," from nurses and doctors alike – some of them nearly in tears.

However, as wonderful as the hospital staff was, I just wanted to go home to heal. I wanted to understand what was happening to me spiritually and why. I also craved mundane experiences like taking a nap on my couch while my son played video games. On November 23rd, I had Thanksgiving dinner with my kids and husband thanks to a dear friend who cooked and delivered the whole meal to my family who then brought it all to the hospital. I was grateful, but still longed to be home. On November 25th, I had a scare where my blood pressure suddenly dropped dangerously low, but the team was able to stabilize me, and my husband was there from the beginning to help me stay calm and in my body. The next morning, I was feeling better and with my husband's help, I was able to make it out of bed and to the sink to brush my teeth and wash my face. My surgeon stopped by my room on his daily check-in and after he left, I resumed my morning hygiene routine with the limited movement required for heart surgery patients. Then I began to feel myself fading and I said to my husband, "It's happening again." He called the doctor and the nurses, and they carried me back to the bed. I could feel myself leaving my body, or more accurately, sinking into myself and away from the outer world. It felt like going to the "sunken place" from the movie *Get Out*, with my view of the world the same as Chris', the main character, with everything and everyone moving further away. My husband stayed directly in front of me, breathing with me while maintaining eye contact and telling me I was going to live. I remember being terrified and thinking repeatedly, "I don't want to die," and even saying it aloud a few times. I remember clearly, it was like I was getting sucked out of this world, but I was fighting to hold on, metaphorically clutching at the walls, with my husband trying to keep me anchored. I recall the force that was pulling me out of this world getting stronger and stronger and my husband says that as he looked in my eyes, he could see the light of my spirit leaving my body. This went on for around 30 minutes or so until…

I died a third time. It was November 26th, 2017 at 10:15am, ten days after the second flatline and eighteen days after the first.

It's unclear how long it took for my heart to beat again. According to my hospital records, I was "coded" for an hour, but I don't think that is feasible. It's more likely that it took that long for the doctors to get my heart going again *and* to stabilize me or the time included the 30 minutes or so that I was fighting to stay in my body. Later that night I was in the operating room again for a third open heart surgery. This time the surgery was exploratory as the doctors searched for answers as to why there was fluid and blood in my pericardium, the sac around my heart. A specialist in bleeding disorders was consulted; they ran tests, and they took my recovery very slowly. This time when I woke up after surgery, I knew I died and survived. I was still intubated with a breathing tube down my throat, feeding tubes in my stomach, and chest tubes draining fluid from my pericardium – not to mention the urinary catheter. I felt like a science experiment. Over the course of the next few days, these tubes were removed, one system at a time. I started the journey to recovery *again*, working with physical and occupational therapists and the rest of the medical team. I heard from even more friends, family, and hospital staff that I was a "walking miracle" and "here for a purpose" and that I "have something important to give." I started to believe them. But what?

In 2016, a year before my health crisis, I had a reading by Chief Oluwo Obafemi Ifayemi and received messages from my ancestors. One of the messages was that my ancestors wanted me to write – for my healing and for theirs as well. I wasn't surprised since my mother always urged me to write when she was alive. However, I did not understand how writing would help my ancestors in the spirit world. Because of that spiritual request and circumstances aligning in my life, I wrote the outline and a draft of the first chapter of this book in the spring of 2017 (more about that in Chapter 1). The other message from 2016 was that they wanted me to learn to finish what I start. At the time, this didn't make a lot of sense to me, but I figured it might later. Both messages resurfaced in my mind as I recovered from my third death and third open heart surgery. I asked the question,

"What am I supposed to do?" Finish what I started.

"What did I start?" You started writing this book and you started healing.

On December 8th, 2017, after fifty days, three deaths, and three open-heart surgeries, I was discharged from the hospital and went home with a spiritual assignment.

It didn't take me long to understand the connection between my life long toxic beliefs and my health crisis. I understood why writing about transformation was critical for my recovery, important for others to hear, and requested by my ancestors. I could also see the importance of a few scientific facts from the American Heart Association that clarified my intent for this book:

- I nearly became one of the 50,000 Black women in America who die each year from heart disease related causes.
- Cardiovascular disease and stroke kill women more than any other cause and disproportionately impacts African-American women.
- Only 36% of African-American women know that heart disease is their greatest health risk and only 1 in

5 African American women believe she is personally at risk.

As well as this point:

- Prolonged trauma modifies DNA through epigenetics and is passed through generations (Lehrner, Yehuda 2018).

As I understood and integrated my experiences along with these facts, I developed a few beliefs:

- I believe that as descendants of enslaved Africans, our ancestors' pain is held spiritually and energetically within our bodies, specifically our hearts.
- I believe that I must heal for my ancestors to heal. The emotional pain I feel is not just my own, but theirs as well.
- I believe that Black people all must heal collectively.

I am here to do this work. I am here to join with others on a transformational journey that is both individual and collective. With this book, I share my revelations from exploring my own toxic core belief and the micro-beliefs that mixed in my mind to create it. I received these micro-beliefs through family and societal influences passed through generations and I dedicate a chapter to each of these. Furthermore, I share the various techniques and practices I use to identify and transform my toxic beliefs through consistent work and commitment.

I believe our ancestors' urgent plea for intergenerational healing, is a call to all descendants of the estimated 450,000 Africans enslaved and dragged to North America and the estimated 12.5 million Africans enslaved throughout the Diaspora (Gates 2014). This is a call to other Black women who may be struggling to reclaim their birthright of health, joy, and success to examine their own thoughts and beliefs. This is a call for Black men who may identify with parts of my story, to reassess their programming and reclaim their birthright as well. Finally, this is a call for anyone of any ethnicity who has an open heart and is willing to step into the trauma, healing, and transformation of my journey and others, to see, feel, and understand a different perspective of life.

And so, I write...

CHAPTER 1

The Belief at the Root of My Pain

"Fat, Black, And Unlovable" are painful words. Actually, they are just words—descriptors or adjectives—used as simple facts or loaded opinions. I was not aware of it, but these words were a part of my internal atmosphere starting in childhood. They amassed a power that permeated my thoughts, influenced my actions, and undermined any effort I made to live a joyous, emotionally balanced, physically healthy life. These words elicited a deep pervasive shame that buried itself in my heart and armored itself from exposure, while over the years building more calluses, shields, and finally, emotional weapons of self-protection. The words were insidious. They hid from light, staying tucked in the corners of my mind, sometimes whispering and other times shouting, doing whatever it took to taint any thoughts or actions that were its opposites. There was a time not long ago that these words consumed my life (and more recently that they nearly *took* my life). The results go by many names— major depression, anxiety, fear, loneliness, insecurity—and their impact on my life was immense.

My parents nor I knew that I was suffering from depression until I was 20 years old. I was home from college for the holidays after another rough semester of isolation and missed classes. My mother had recently read an article about depression and insisted I see a psychologist. The doctor said the signs and symptoms were clear and diagnosed me with major depression.

Finally, we had a name for what I had been struggling with since I was a kid. Mental health wasn't something my parents considered when I periodically withdrew from activities and people. Nor was it top of mind when I steadily gained weight or had anxiety attacks, and not even when I attempted suicide as a teen. Like many in the Black community back then, my parents did not know much about mental health or what to do about it. Turns out, I had a real problem, not just personality quirks, and it had a name: depression.

However, knowing I struggled with depression didn't magically reveal the cause or free me from its grip. When I returned to school after the diagnosis, I started seeing the school therapist and learned about the process of emotions and behaviors stemming from thoughts. I began to understand that if I wanted to feel better, I had to think better thoughts. But my thoughts seemed to have a life of their own, reacting negatively to whatever stimulus I encountered. It took years to be able to slow down the mental chatter enough to recognize the individual thoughts and link them to feelings of anxiety or despair. I improved my thought awareness through journaling and talk therapy. I spent many a night furiously writing whatever came to mind with no filter or evaluation – just providing an outlet for the thoughts that were circulating in my mind. When I met with my therapist (I had several over the years), we would talk about a specific and current dilemma in my life to help me identify what I was feeling and thinking in the situation. It was a slow process and only the first stage of *recognizing* my thoughts before I could make any successful attempts to *change* my thoughts. I tried for years to gain control over my ruminations to uplift myself from anxiety and depression. I attempted to replace harsh thoughts like "I'm stupid and always messing up my life," with more compassionate ones like "I'm doing ok and I can do even better." Still, it was like my mind had its own ideas about me and my life that could not be changed. Thus, many years of intermittent therapy only resulted in incremental changes over time, not the seismic shift I needed to be healthy.

When I wasn't working through a major depression episode, my therapy sessions explored the idea of core beliefs. Intellectually, I understood core beliefs as the collective lens through which we see ourselves and experience the world, but it remained an abstraction for me. I didn't spend much time exploring my thoughts to find their root beliefs. By this time, I was a single working mother who was usually experiencing some level of depression. Functioning through the pain to care for my child and put a roof over our heads left me with little interest in working on my mental health. However, experiencing my beliefs, thoughts, and emotions for my daughter helped me begin to understand my core beliefs about myself. I *believed* my daughter was my number one priority so of course I *thought* about making sure she was happy and safe, *felt* unconditional love for her, then *did* things I thought would ensure she felt loved, safe and happy. By looking at the pathway from belief to thought to emotion and action regarding my daughter, I started to trace my self-talk and thoughts back to beliefs about myself. Beliefs don't always work that linearly, but they are the seeds that produce stalks of thoughts which bear the fruit of emotions and behaviors.

The combined strategy of journaling and talk therapy helped me identify persistent beliefs like: "People will always hurt me if I let them," "I am a failure," or "No one will ever love me," as the seeds, I needed to uproot. As hard as it was and for as long as it took, identifying my thoughts and beliefs was the easy part. I went to work doing the things I thought would help—saying affirmations, reading self-help books, and trying different therapeutic approaches. Throughout my time in therapy working to change my core beliefs, my goal was to feel better emotionally and rid myself of depressed and anxious emotional states. I traced the path of my thoughts to my beliefs, but I didn't consider my resulting behaviors other than my tendency to isolate and drop out of activities when I was in a depression episode. I didn't consider that for weeks or months at time, I did nothing to strengthen and fortify myself physically. The body is meant to move, and the heart is meant to pump, but I spent a lot of time unable to muster the energy to do anything above the bare minimum. Thus, a sedentary lifestyle became the norm for me. Yet despite the lethargy I felt episodically throughout my life, I was still so anxious that I numbed myself with cigarettes, food, TV, and romance novels. Because of my inability to appropriately self-care, I experienced escalating health problems such as continuous weight gain, systemic inflammation, recurring debilitating migraines, a weakened immune system, and high blood pressure. I knew I shouldn't smoke, but it soothed my nerves. I learned what foods were not good for me and how I needed to eat to be a healthy weight, but self-care for me meant eating whatever triggered a release of dopamine and felt good in the moment. This was usually high sodium, high fat, and high carb foods. Things that distracted me, like TV and romance novels, all seemed like must haves to ensure I was having "me time." Moreover, my body not only responded to my lifestyle choices, but to my emotional state as well. Chronic stress exhausted my endocrine system throwing my hormones out of balance, further contributing to my subpar health and mood. Heavy periods and PMS as well as insomnia and chronic fatigue were a few more manifestations of a body in crisis. While I was fighting to change my beliefs and thoughts to escape the grips of depression and anxiety, my body was taking the punches and enduring the pain.

I did not know that I was only flailing around in shallow surface water never reaching the depths of my emotional ocean. I was attempting to change beliefs that were simply the offspring of the mother belief. I was trying to plant new seeds in toxic soil. Every time I thought I made progress on changing my beliefs, other negative thoughts of the same energy as the one I just "eliminated" would pop up. It was an exhausting game of whack-a-mole that felt impossible to win. My hidden core belief fed and regenerated my moles and gained its power by hiding and diverting my thought energy. It was a no-win situation.

However, it was not until I was forty-five that my mind was clear enough to hear what was whispering to me most of my life, "Fat, Black, and Unlovable."

I took a break from my corporate career and stepped away from an executive nonprofit role. My oldest child was soon graduating from college and my youngest child was becoming an independent teenager. Intimacy and connection with my husband were at an all-time low and our marriage seemed to be ending. With fewer life distractions, an emptying nest, and a declining marriage, I began to explore my own needs. I always loved dance, so I was taking authentic Afro-Brazilian dance classes and noticing the similarities between African-American and Afro-Brazilian culture, feeling a kindred connection with Black people in Brazil. Every year my dance teacher and Brazilian native taught the rhythms and dances of different Òrìṣà (also spelled Orisha or Orixa). Òrìṣà are personified representations of forces of nature in one of the spiritual traditions brought to Brazil by Africans forced there in chains. It is called Candomblé and has a similar pantheon of deities and set of practices as many traditional spiritual systems throughout the Diaspora and Africa. The dances were beautiful and told the story of each deity and the energy they represent. I also experienced and was studying sacred sexuality and various energy healing modalities, so I was open to non-mainstream spiritual practices. Still, it wasn't until our teacher introduced our class to Oṣùn (also spelled Oshun, Ochun, or Oxum) that something in me stood up and took notice. Oṣùn is the goddess of fresh waters, love and sensuality and I connected with her movements and concepts more than any other Òrìṣà dance we practiced. I was intrigued by Oṣùn 's promise to bring sweetness to one's life but confused as to why she was associated with mirrors. I wanted to learn more and as they say, when the student is ready, the teacher will appear—

spiritually and in physical form. Turns out a woman I had known for a few years, as a frequent client in her spa, was a priestess in a spiritual tradition like Candomblé, called Ifa. I was able to ask her questions and receive guidance on personal practices like connecting with nature and venerating my ancestors, as well as books to read on African spiritual traditions. I am eternally grateful to her for introducing me to Ifa and sharing her knowledge. She taught me that we each have an Òrìṣà that walks with us to assist us on our journey, and I was drawn to Oṣùn because she is the Òrìṣà who walks with me. Through study, I learned that Oṣùn is associated with mirrors not because of vanity (though she does love beautiful things), but because she encourages healing through self-reflection and improvement.

The more I learned about Ifa, the more familiar it felt. I started to see my life as a journey back to myself, back to the path of destiny I chose before my birth, and back to the spiritual practices of my ancestors. When I was a child, I would often cry, sobbing "I want to go home." I can clearly remember the deep emotions I used to feel: sad, lost, and alone. This memory stayed with me for forty years and I would periodically think about these moments in my young life. I can't recall how many times it happened, but I get the sense that it was only a few. It was puzzling because I would have these moments while at home, in the same house I was born and raised in, and with my family including my parents. I wasn't abused or neglected. I just really wanted *something* but did not understand what it was or how else to articulate it. But whatever it was, a place or a time or a state of being, I knew it was where I was supposed to be and to be apart from it hurt.

I believe that longing was for awareness of and a conscious connection with the deepest part of myself. I believe that longing was my desire to reignite in my spirit that which was growing dormant as I was programmed into my family and society. I believe that longing was the seed of divine love taking root, despite the toxic soil of beliefs I was nurturing, so that as a child of my ancestors, I would not be lost. This longing gave me something to ponder, something to seek out so that the sadness, anger, shame, and guilt I absorbed would not take me and I would remember my destiny. That seed of divine love helped me receive messages through my dreams rather than disregard them. That seed gave me clarity early in life that Abrahamic religions, while confirming my belief in Spirit, were not enough for me. That seed survived all these years, protecting and guiding me through the trials of life to a path of growth and wisdom. As I learned more about Ifa, I could feel the seed and understand it more than I did as a child. Sadness and longing were slowly replaced with peaceful excitement and a desire for more. I wanted to nurture that seed and experience how it could grow and manifest in my life. I knew that studying nature through Ifa would nurture that seed of divine love, giving me greater understanding and vision. Then the most important catalyst on my journey to transformation happened when I decided to walk the path of Ifa. I participated in a ceremony called Isefa and became an abọriṣà, a student of nature. I answered the call of my Ancestral Mothers and accepted my contract with destiny. Things in my life began to change.

Soon after my Isefa, our ile (spiritual group or congregation) announced a trip to Salvador, Bahia, Brazil, the same city my dance instructor was from and a place I had wanted to visit for years. Bahia was the epicenter of the slave trade in Brazil and the entry point for the millions of enslaved Africans brought there by the Portuguese. I decided to not only go on the group trip, but to head there a week early to take intensive dance classes and experience the soul of Bahia on my own. Because of my plans, I was determined to drop some pounds so that two hours of dance class five days a week while in Brazil would not break me! Oddly enough I was starting to lose weight doing things I had done dozens of times before with no success. The only difference was my new connection to Ifa and the deeper relationship I was cultivating with my ancestors. I was learning to listen to my body, to feed it when it was hungry and to stop eating when it was satisfied. Because of working with the Òrìṣà and my Ègún (ancestors), my mind and nervous system were calm enough to see when my habit of eating was in direct response to my emotions, regardless of hunger. I was forced to address my feelings. I also did not have the pressure of family or work responsibilities "preventing" me from exercising, triggering stress eating, or distracting me from experiencing my feelings. I saw the scale going down, but that was just a data point and not real to me. Then some of my clothes became too big, my bras were loose, and the section of my closet with clothes I have had for years, but never wore because I bought them for "when I lose weight", were suddenly fitting. I realized that I was getting smaller! I lost 40lbs, however, when I looked in the mirror, I could not see any change. I stared in the full-length mirror regularly—sometimes naked, sometimes wearing some outfit that finally fit—looking for the change, searching for the amazing feeling I thought I would get when the pounds finally started to come off. However, it did not come. What came was "Fat, Black, and Unlovable." I realized that no matter how much weight I lost, how rich my life was, how happy my kids were, how attentive my husband used to be, how many friends I had, how successful and smart I appeared to be, I would always look in the mirror and see myself as "Fat, Black, and Unlovable." That is unless I transformed this toxic belief into nourishing soil that would produce healthy thoughts, emotions, and behaviors. This toxin permeated the soil of my mind. This was the hidden core belief that fed and regenerated my negative self-beliefs and gained its power by hiding amidst my ego. In order to dismantle this belief, I first had to clearly define these words.

"Fat" can mean having excess body fat or being substantial, impressive, or profitable. Somehow, it had become an insult and a source of shame for me. Recent body positive movements embrace the word as simply an adjective devoid of its negative connotations. However, in my life, "fat" was only used as a sharp blade meant to cut down and cause pain and it cut far too deeply to simply flip it and use it. I had to transform and replace this word to hear something different and see my true self when I looked in the mirror.

According to Webster, "Black" has many definitions that refer to everything from simply a pigment to people of African descent, but most of the definitions have negative connotations such as sad, gloomy, sinister, evil, and dirty. Despite these implied definitions, this is a word that I thought I used with my own understanding of what it meant. For me, to say, "I am Black" is a distinction that unites me with people of color all over the globe—particularly historically oppressed people with African ancestry. Yes, I am an African-American, but to me that is a geographical description of origin and circumstance. To be Black is much richer and more meaningful. It is a source of pride and culture. Still, as a Black woman I have carried a sense of shame about being Black. My undeniable African features—dark brown skin and kinky hair with full lips, hips, and butt—I embraced while at the same time feeling less beautiful, less desirable, and less attractive because of them. As such, I had to reach deeper into the thoughts and feelings of being Black to eradicate the shame and find my true essence.

"Unlovable" has the simplest dictionary definition of all with no duality or spectrum of meaning—not having attractive or appealing qualities that would inspire admiration or affection. Wow! How does one cope with that? I can tell you what I have done. I have looked everywhere outside of myself for evidence that I could be loved. I tested the love of others, tried to read the degree and sincerity of love received, demanded proof and confirmation of love repeatedly, withheld love from others and myself, and rejected love. Since I really did not believe that I could be loved, my tolerance for vulnerability was near zero and relationships would become heavy and difficult once the initial euphoria of "being in love" or new relationship energy wore off.

Not knowing all along that I would never experience receiving, giving, or personifying the love I so desperately wanted until I could love myself and truly know love. "Unlovable" was a contaminant that seeped into the ground to destroy any attempts of nurturing a vibrant emotional garden. It had to go.

Through her mirror of self-reflection, Oṣùn, the Òrìṣà who walks with me, revealed the lie I had been telling myself, yet she also revealed the truth. Yeye Oṣùn showed me that while I saw "Fat, Black, and Unlovable" in the mirror, my truth is "Beautiful. Powerful. Love." Knowing where my truth lay inspired me, but didn't magically transport me there, I had to work at it continuously. My Ègún (ancestors) and the Òrìṣà opened the way, showed me the path, and gave me the tools, but I had to do the soul work to remove the toxins from my soil. Hence, I went back to what had helped me before, I started writing. At first, I wrote about this core belief of "Fat Black and Unlovable" from the perspective of my struggle with weight loss. I journaled a stream of consciousness which quickly became a mental word battle with my ego, who promptly let me know that I still had a long way to my goal weight so what right did I have to write?! Then I stopped writing. Nonetheless, I had already started to awaken. The seed of divine love that survived in me all those years was growing and cleansing the soil of my consciousness. The next few months would bring experiences and awareness, highs and lows that would pierce through the veil and force me to confront this belief head on. Either this core belief would consume me, swallow me whole, and digest me slowly and painfully like victims of the sand creature from *Return of the Jedi* or I would dismantle and dissolve it, starting a new life free from its constant shackles and abuse.

I discovered that I did not have to be controlled by this lie. I had a choice and I chose victory over this belief. I chose its death and the death of my former self that was ruled by this lie. I chose love. I chose life. Even as my heart stopped, and I left my body three times, I chose to do the work to transform this belief and free my spirit in this lifetime rather than waiting for the next.

I asked myself where did the belief, "Fat, Black, and Unlovable," come from? How could I reverse the damage to my health from decades of emotional and mental stress, negative thoughts, and unhealthy decisions? The change I needed was too massive to "positive think" my way to the major transformation my body demanded, and my soul yearned for. Then I came across a TEDTalk featuring Dr. Brené Brown, a social work researcher and professor at the University of Houston. Brown's talk was about her research on the impact of shame and vulnerability in our lives and strategies to overcome it. I began to look more into her work and found an Audible recording of a seminar she held that combined all her work on shame, vulnerability, authenticity and connection – *The Power of Vulnerability*. As I listened to her points validated by research and personal antidotes, I sat with the ideas and just let them marinate. What resulted was a framework to break my core belief down into components. I examined what I learned from my family of origin along with beliefs that were implanted and reinforced by society and discovered micro-beliefs that merged to create the toxic soil that was "Fat, Black, and Unlovable." This book is about my discoveries through self-reflection and mental, emotional excavation to trace the path of "Fat, Black, and Unlovable," to its predecessors among family and society mindsets.

Delving deeper into my earliest beliefs instilled through my family, I realized that some of these ideas were passed down through generations, dating back to the times of our enslavement. I explore these influential ideas in Chapter 2: *Plantation Proverbs*. I believe it is through these "Plantation Proverbs" that my ancestors left clues to the psychological and spiritual wounds that I have carried in my own body and mind and need to heal for myself and my bloodline. By stepping into the micro beliefs, the little building blocks that created "Fat, Black, and Unlovable," I see its origin extending into the past, before my birth, steeped in the pain and sorrows of slavery and its aftermath. Epigeneticists study how exposure to prolonged trauma leaves its traces in our DNA and is passed from parents to children. Researchers in the field of epigenetics, Dr. Rachel Yehuda of the Icahn School of Medicine at Mount Sinai, MSSM Department of Psychiatry and Dr. Amy Lehrner of James J. Peters Veterans Affairs Medical Center, have published several articles indicating the evidence that trauma passes genetically from generation to generation. Considering the slave trade across the entire Diaspora, the trauma of slavery was a 500-year nightmare that still impacts Black people physically and emotionally today. Furthermore, regarding intergenerational transference of trauma, **Yehuda and Lehrner agree** that "…the role of community-level processes for healing" is critical. In other words, all descendants of enslaved Africans must heal and must do it as a community. In Ifa, the African spiritual tradition that I practice, ancestral veneration is a central component as our ancestors guide and protect us spiritually. I believe we are reborn (reincarnated) through our bloodline, and I work with my ancestors to improve my life today and improve their lives upon their eventual return as my children and my grandchildren and so on. This makes our experience of trauma from previous generations not only a scientifically proven genetic inheritance, but a spiritual/energetic endowment as well.

'Plantation Proverbs" were only one ingredient in the toxic belief of "Fat, Black, and Unlovable." Media and societal influences also contributed to my negative view of myself, leaving me with the belief that I would never be successful, beautiful, lovable, or desirable. I investigate this notion further in Chapter 3: *Mammies and Jezebels*. Through mass media like books, movies, and television, stereotypes of Black women were perpetuated ever since the first European colonists invaded Africa. Many of these hurtful one-dimensional depictions of Black women were developed as a justification for slavery and the rape culture that surrounded it. Other more modern stereotypes contributed to the rift in the Black community, including the relationship between Black men and Black women. The hopes, joys, and fears of our Ancestral Mothers and Fathers have been nearly obliterated from our consciousness as many Black women struggle to shed the colonizer's definition of us.

As stated, we often inherit our aversion to vulnerability from our parents as well as our methods to avoid it. I have found myself enduring similar mental and physical health issues as my mother. As I examined the "Plantation Proverbs" and stereotypes of Black women, I realize that my mother's life was even more directly impacted by these concepts. While my health crisis could have been mitigated by healthy lifestyle choices earlier in my life, mental transformation was just as critical. I must do the work to change my beliefs and free my mind, for myself, my mother, and my children. I share some of the techniques I use to heal and transform my mind in Chapter 4: *Transformation Ain't Easy.*

Our ancestors are the past, our children are the future, and we are the connecting link. If our children are to be elevated and realize the joy, peace, and success that is their birthright, then we must heal. If our ancestors are to rejoice in the physical freedom we have achieved, as well as the emotional and spiritual liberation needed to create the good condition on earth, together we must do the work to heal.

CHAPTER 2

Plantation Proverbs: Surviving Enslavement

As I worked on my healing, I realized that my self-belief of being "Fat, Black, and Unlovable" was saturated with fear and shame. In Dr. Brené Brown's *Power of Vulnerability*, the researcher explains that the constructs that create shame can often be found in what our parents modeled for us as children. While everyone can grow beyond his or her childhood influences, quite often we find ourselves repeating the words and actions displayed to us as kids—even if we vowed, we never would. The intention of these statements can be timeless words of wisdom, admonishments of risky behavior, or encouraging keys to success. This passing down of guidance can continue until it propagates seven or more generations into the future. I believe this continuity of guidance was key to our survival as descendants of enslaved Africans, helping us build on the experiences of others to help keep us safe in a hostile world. During slavery and Jim Crow, the guidance passed on to children in our lineages for safety and survival has now become a swirling concoction of beliefs, misinterpreted by more recent generations and applied erroneously to a different era. I call these "Plantation Proverbs," and they were passed down out of hope, love, and fear. The phrases I discuss here were words I heard as a child from my parents and elders in my family. These words, and many others, were necessary lessons we had to learn to survive the brutality of slavery and its cousin, Jim Crow. The children of enslaved adults were urged to heed these warnings in hopes of increasing the odds that they would survive to be adults themselves. As modern descendants of this legacy, we all internalize these proverbs in our own way as they mix with unique aspects of our individual mental and emotional make-up.

"Plantation Proverbs" exemplifies what my parents modeled for me, and what was modeled for them and so on. "Fat, Black, and Unlovable" has its roots in the proverbs spoken by my parents, grandparents, aunts, and uncles and these roots run deep, passing through previous generations that may have been simultaneously protected and yet damaged by them. I owe it to my bloodline to examine the wisdom and warnings within each admonishment to understand the context in which the proverb was created, unpack how my young mind internalized it, and reframe it to be more relevant and empowering now. What follows is my assessment of five "Plantation Proverbs" that had the greatest impact on my beliefs and the formation of "Fat, Black and Unlovable."

"The empty wagon rattles loud goin' down the road"

Many people have used the phrase for enough years that it is truly considered a proverb. Do a quick internet search and you will find Plato credited with the original of version of this phrase. One will also find different interpretations; sometimes the empty wagon is a shallow person or a person who knows nothing. In either case, rattling loudly down the road is that person talking a lot, usually to mask their lack of knowledge. I heard this often from my parents when I was growing up. My parents explained how when picking cotton back home in Mississippi, the wagon would make loud irritating rattling sounds as it made its way through the cotton fields calling attention to the approaching wagon. After a day's work, the wagon would be full and heavy with cotton, barely making a sound as it traveled back down the road, away from the fields and toward the main house for weighing and processing.

This very culturally relevant interpretation of the phrase is something my parents undoubtedly heard and experienced when they were children. It stemmed from the time of slavery when an empty or even light wagon meant another backbreaking day of work or violent abuse for not meeting the ever-rising quotas. An empty wagon meant pain and suffering. Many enslaved Africans did what they could to protect their children and teach them how to survive—fill the wagon, make the quota, stay quiet and unnoticed, and avoid the wrath of the overseer's whip. Although my parents were not enslaved, they did sharecrop and pick cotton with many of the same anxieties and grew-up on or near the same plantations upon which our ancestors were enslaved. This tale of caution was passed down as a technique of survival from times of enslavement to sharecropping to being Black in modern America. My parents heard it as children and given the nearby murder of Emmett Till when they were young adults in Mississippi, staying under the radar was still a relevant survival technique when they started their family. Of course, as parents who lost their only son in what they suspected as a racially motivated incident (more about that later), they would do everything they could to protect their children and prepare them to survive in the world. Do not be an empty wagon. Know what you are talking about before you speak. Only speak what demonstrates your knowledge or makes a point. Don't be overly joyful or loud. Survive and live.

Times have changed, but they have not. A Black person who draws the attention of some white people is still a person in possible danger. Black men are still murdered by racist police officers and in many parts of this country (and the world), it is still dangerous to be Black and bring attention to yourself. Michael Brown was shot to death by a white police officer in Ferguson, Missouri; Eric Garner died after being placed in a chokehold by NYPD officers; Dontre Hamilton was fatally shot 14 times by a police officer in Milwaukee; and Rumain Brisbon was shot and killed by a Phoenix police officer—are a few examples from just 2014.

Despite my struggles with depression early in life, I was still considered gregarious, whether I was all out dancing when my jam came on the radio in the car or breaking out in a dance move when I got excited about something. My natural response to joy was usually one that could draw attention. Looking back with the knowledge that love of dance is embodied in the energy of Ọṣùn , my guiding Òrìṣà, it is not surprising that dance would be both my joy trigger and response. It was usually after one of these times that my parents would caution me about the empty wagon. They were warning me that certain behavior would indicate to people that I was not intelligent or was foolish in some way. In general, it was best to avoid this perception so one should abstain from talking when you aren't certain of your correctness. However, it seemed to me, to guarantee my safety, I should avoid doing *anything* that would call attention to myself unless I was certain of my own perfection.

In my life, this threat has been much more nuanced, making the effects of a low profile much less about protection and more about confinement. I did not grow up in the South nor have I ever picked cotton. I have never felt like my life was in danger due to racial violence. However, I have felt that my voice, thoughts, opinions, or intuition did not matter and that my knowledge and intellect were more important yet still had to be proven. The first time I can remember this belief making its first impression on me was in first grade. I was five years old and promoted to 1st grade after only two weeks in kindergarten. It is amazing how simple experiences can become emotional and forever seeped in our memory. The teacher asked each student to make the sound of the first letter of the animal she showed. When it was my turn, she showed me a picture of a cow. I said, very proudly because I *knew* I was right, "Mooooo!" I was so nervous to be in a new class with older kids that I thought I was supposed make the sound of the animal in the picture not the word. Of course, the class laughed, and the teacher said, "No, [say] the word," with a gentle chuckle. I was devastated but managed to make my hard "C" sound anyway. The empty wagon rattled.

The next time the empty wagon proverb was reinforced, I was in 5th grade and attending a magnet school with gifted kids of various ethnicities from all over the Southside of Chicago. Everyone was smart, and many knew more about the world than I did. There was one class module about Europe and each kid had to give a presentation about what country they would like to visit or had already visited and why they chose it. Many kids had already been to France, Italy, or England, but I had never even been on an airplane. Despite my limited experience, I felt confident about talking about traveling. Our family took one or two vacations every year which was more than any of the kids at my old school. I felt lucky and privileged in that regard until I heard people talking about visiting other countries—places I wasn't quite sure where they were located on the map. When it was my turn, I leaned into what I knew. I talked about wanting to take a road trip to Paris! Of course, many kids laughed and one kid (there is always that one who wants to show how much they know) said mockingly, "You can't drive to Paris!" I was confused. On all the vacations that I took with my family we drove in a station wagon, van, or RV. Why couldn't we drive to France? My family had taken a road trip to Niagara Falls and that was in another country! Then one kid (there is always a savior too) said, "You could if you go across Alaska to Russia and keep heading west!" They proceeded to argue for a minute until the teacher hushed them. By this time, the damage was done—I was the empty wagon. Not only did I not know that I could not drive to France, but I did not even know where Alaska was in relation to Russia and France to defend myself in the argument the boys were having. For the next couple of years, I would not raise my hand in school and would sometimes freeze while giving mandatory presentations. Without this underlying belief about being an empty wagon, both situations could have been funny little blips in the past that I may not even remember. Instead, these early incidents confirmed that opening my mouth put me at risk to be perceived as an empty wagon. From that point forward, I would contemplate whatever I was about to say in any situation – school, work, or social – usually for so long that I missed the opportunity to participate in the discussion at all. Looking back, I can attribute much of my behavior to fear of being labeled as an empty wagon. I would observe people around me to assess my environment as well as my understanding and ability to make meaningful contributions before I engage. This played out early in my career when I would not speak up in meetings or offer insights or opinions out of fear of being the empty wagon. This fear showed up in my relationships as well. There was a time when I couldn't have a meaningful conversation and share my point of view—if I couldn't *prove* my point, I remained silent.

Today I no longer live in fear of being the empty wagon. Instead, I strive to "Be prepared, be present, be aware." To support this transformation, I apply *The Work* described in Chapter 4.

"Do as I say, not as I do"

This phrase, like several of these "Plantation Proverbs," is not exclusive to Black people or created only from observations of our circumstances. Historically, "Do as I say, not as I do" is associated with hypocrisy and the idea that people tell you to do one thing while their own behavior displays the opposite. For my people, I believe the hypocrisy was that of our ancestors' enslavers. I imagine it to have been words barked by overseers and slave owners to demonstrate their control over the subjugated. I can hear preachers spouting this rhetoric within the guise of religion as a means to justify the practice of slavery and encourage enslaved Africans to accept their lot. The message? "Don't talk back, don't think, and don't try to assert your freedom as if you are a white man. Just be obedient and accept bondage."

I can also imagine our kin hearing these words and adapting them for their needs as they have done repeatedly in various ways and circumstances. I believe that when our people spoke these words, the theme was survival rather than hypocrisy. Our ancestors needed to ensure their children would heed their warnings to avoid being sold away, beaten, raped, or murdered. As we know from well-documented slave escape systems, often instructions and plans were embedded in songs or stories. Perhaps "Do as I say" was a means of preparing children to listen for messages encoded in the words of the adults. Alternatively, perhaps the intention was around safety rather than eventual escape or revolt. Every moment of an enslaved person's life was tenuous at best and required adults to take risky actions to ensure the continuity of the bloodline. Whether it was secretly learning to read, sharing information, or hiding supplies, adults were willing to take calculated risks that they would not want their children to take. Thus, "Do as I say" could have evolved to warn children not to emulate the risks they may have seen the adults taking. Lastly, when our great-great-grandparents used these phrases, the intention could have been more inspirational. Plantation life was inhumane and brutal, but our ancestors survived it, in large part, because of the love and faith infused into their DNA. That love and faith would prompt them to encourage their children to aspire to do more than their parents, in order to build, grow, and overcome. Whether our ancestors transformed these words for purposes of espionage, preservation, or motivation, the overarching purpose was survival of the bloodline.

Fast forward to the second wave of the Great Migration from 1940 to 1970 when over three and a half million Blacks folks left the south and headed north for better opportunities. Descendants of former slaves from Mississippi, Alabama, and some from Louisiana traveled north and ended up in the Midwest like my parents and brought with them, "Plantation Proverbs." "Do as I say" is a sentiment that many Black or southern folks I grew up around in Chicago heard regularly. I honestly cannot recall how often they said the phrase directly to me, but my parents told us kids how we needed to live, how we needed to act, or advised us on avoiding mistakes they learned from experience. They wanted us to have an easier and better life than they did. However, there was a disconnect between the teachings of my parents, specifically my mother, and what she modeled. She told her daughters to be strong, smart, and independent and she did that with her words and by example. She also told me to be happy and love myself, but from what I observed, my mother was often anxious, sometimes depressed, and struggled to love all aspects of herself.

My mother was born in 1937 in Mississippi, the youngest of ten girls. Her mother died before she was two years old, so her father, stepmother, and older sisters raised her. It was not clear how my grandmother died given the limited access to medical care they had in rural Mississippi. When I was growing up, I recall hushed talk among my aunts that their mother may have taken her own life (someone saw her take something before she died). Recently, I learned that my grandmother died in childbirth having her eleventh child and who would have been her only son. In any case, after bringing ten girls into the world, my grandmother made her transition leaving my mother to grow up without her love and care. My mother was a beautiful, sought-after teenager, tall, light-skinned (as was and often still is preferred due to colorism in the Black community) with an hourglass figure. She played basketball, did well in school, and was outspoken. She met my father as a teenager and would often say he was like her knight in shining armor, which I always thought that was so beautiful. However, I never thought to ask, what was he was saving her from since knights are typically saving a damsel in distress? The few pictures of my mother when she was a teen reflect a bit of sadness in her eyes. Years later, some of the things my parents would argue over, seemed, at its root, to be about my father not loving her the way she needed or wanted to be loved.

She would often say he would do anything for us kids and do anything for others to be the "good guy" to people but did not go out of his way for her. As the eavesdropping kid, it was never clear to me what she needed; from my perspective and conversations with my dad, he loved my mother beyond measure. He would always say she was the brains of their business partnership and the way he looked *at* her, spoke about her, and spoke *to* her – was filled with love and respect.

Looking back, I realize that as amazing, smart, and beautiful as my mother was, she did not see herself that way. As the youngest child who spent a lot of time at her hip, I often noticed a sadness in her eyes. She could cook her ass off, worked harder than anyone I have ever known, was compassionate and kind, loved to dance and travel, and loved and supported her children with an unshakable certainty. She ALWAYS looked and smelled good, was beautiful and sexy, all while carrying herself with the regality of a queen. Yet, she struggled to love and accept herself fully. Compassion, love, and support was something she gave to others, but rarely directed it internally to herself. She would reprimand us for making fun of or criticizing other people, but I often heard my mother harshly criticize herself. She was a beautiful voluptuous woman, who many men desired—old, young, it didn't matter. I witnessed boys and men half my mother's age, double take and stare at her as she walked by and yet she compared herself to and envied other women all the time. These were the only times she judged others—after comparing herself to someone and feeling less than—a typical response to the treat of shame and vulnerability according to Brené Brown's research shared in the *Power of Vulnerability*.

Furthermore, depression plagued my mother as well. Back in the day, my parents had a canopy bed with lace curtains surrounding it—very Arabian nights. When I was young, maybe around seven, I vividly recall my mother being on the edge of the bed in her nightgown looking very sad with an absent look. She lit the lace curtains on fire and just sat there. I remember my sisters yelling and screaming, I think my father came from another part of the house and put the fire out, but not before it burned the sheets and scorched the mattress. I can still see her sitting there surrounded by the burning curtain. However, other details are very fuzzy, as I was shuttled away so I would not see much. My parents kept that mattress for years and I always saw the burn marks and remembered what happened, but never understood why. In my family, you learned early not to pry into grown folks' business or bring up embarrassing or painful questions, so I never asked. What was she thinking? What triggered the pain she felt? What was so bad that she wanted to give up on life? What had someone, even me, done to her? I never knew and since I cannot physically ask her now, I may never know for certain.

The parallels between my mother's emotional states and the thoughts and feelings I had about myself are staggering, right down to the suicide attempts. By the time I was 19, I had attempted suicide at least three times. The first attempt was in my early teens when I slit my wrists in response to a deep hopelessness I felt. It seemed to me that I was not pretty; I wasn't smart enough, and I didn't matter so I wasn't worth being alive. My second suicide attempt was a few years later when I took a package of over the counter sleeping pills in response to feeling overwhelmingly unloved—this time by my boyfriend. I have vague memories of attempting to end my life with sleeping pills another time, but I cannot recall the actual circumstance of it. The last attempt—more of a narrow escape—I can clearly recall was when I was 19 years old. I sat in my car at a crossroad of a main throughway in Chicago that was frequented late at night by high-speed 18-wheel trucks. I sat there longing to floor the gas and rush into the path of one of the oncoming speeding trucks. I sat there for hours feeling unloved and hopeless; trying to get what I thought was courage to press the gas pedal. In each of those attempts to end my life, I believe I was saved by my ancestors and my own higher consciousness who have always supported and protected me long before I was aware of their existence. I was never hospitalized or seriously injured; the wrist cuts were not deep enough to bleed out. They only left scars which have now faded 30 years later. The sleeping pills were not strong enough to render me unconscious or stop my heart, only over stimulate my nervous system, sending me into a purgatory of agitated lethargy. The tragic thought of my parents' pain if they lost their youngest child who was born in honor of a departed sibling, if I died in a violent truck crash, made the lure of ending my life too selfish to go forward. Thus, I drove home and went to bed. Since those days of my youth, I experienced suicidal thoughts again, in small ways, but my love for and from my children always gave me the strength to push through whatever momentary pain I felt. Until about 2010 or 2011, after a few years of functioning through major depression and dysthymia, I felt that I was no good to anyone—my job or my family. I even rationalized that my children would be better without me, reasoning that they would heal from the temporary sadness of losing me but be happier in the end. So, I drove to the mountains, unsure of why or what I intended to do. I found a trailhead nestled between mountains and parked. I cried for hours, asking God what the point was. Why was I here? Why did I exist? What good am I? I can see it clearly in my mind now: it was a glorious sunny day, the sky was clear and deep blue, and the mountains were beautiful and majestic, covered with trees and foliage. High among the mountaintops I could see huge eagles soaring around surveying the land, doing what they do with the brilliant blue sky as their backdrop. I noticed the trees swaying in the wind, some leaves falling, others remained attached, but danced with the breeze. I became aware of the mountains themselves—huge, ancient, unmovable, deceptively inactive, yet teeming with life and energy. Suddenly I was overwhelmed with a thought, "You are here to witness." This incredibly dynamic and timeless display of nature needed me and only asked that I witness it, that I witness life. I did not have to be a thing, do a thing, or give anything except my awareness, to be present. Then my tears were no longer of sorrow and despair, but of surrender and gratitude. I was accepted, and I did not have to offer anything in return. I was healed enough to return home to my family and to a therapist for the next few years to begin my healing again. I was ready to do as my mother said and not only as she did. I was ready to learn how to be happy and to love and accept myself.

"Always expect the worst"

I heard this from both my parents throughout my entire life. It was not always those exact words, but the sentiment was always there. People will hurt you, do you wrong, and be out to get you. In all fairness, they also said, "When life hands you lemons, make lemonade." However, the idea that life has sour lemons was always there. As I mentioned, my parents were born in the 30's in Mississippi where they were raised amidst harsh racism and oppression. For many Black people in America, then and now, things did and do go wrong, making fear and disappointment a constant possibility. Even when things were good, there was always something around the corner waiting to threaten or destroy your happiness. Enslaved Africans in Mississippi endured some of the most brutal and inhumane conditions in North America. According to Gene Dattel in *Cotton and Race in the Making of America,* Mississippi went from having no cotton industry when it became a state in 1817 to producing over 535 million pounds of cotton in 1859, quickly becoming the highest cotton producing state in America. During that time, the U.S. population of enslaved Africans went from less than 4,000 to just under a half million with enslaved labor not only picking cotton, but also supporting all facets of plantation life as tanners, shoemakers, blacksmiths, carpenters, millers, maids, cooks, seamstresses, and nursemaids, etc., all with no payment and amidst brutal conditions. Mississippi was at the epicenter of the great global demand for cotton, so plantation owners hired "overseers" to manage the workers in the field and maximize output. Many of these overseers were poor uneducated white men who exacted cruel torture upon the enslaved. The boney remains of former slaves tell the story of extreme abuse and wear from heavy cotton bales of constantly rising weight and back-breaking plantation work. Like the enslaved everywhere, life for enslaved Africans there was bleak and filled with emotional and physical pain. Many did not survive and those that did had to find a way to deal with inevitability of being beaten, maimed, raped, or lynched at any moment. There was also the knowledge that their mate or children could experience any of those things or be sold away and never seen again. Some managed mentally by becoming as complacent and docile as possible and taught this to their children as a path to survival. Others locked away their hopes and joy like a treasure to safeguard and lived a life of constant precaution, accepting and embracing the certainty of bad things happening. All these survival techniques were passed to successive generations by direct communication, observations, and frankly, genetics. Pregnant women were not immune to the horrific impact of slavery – overseers would often dig a hole large enough for a woman's pregnant belly to rest in the ground, while she lay on her stomach, and was beaten with a whip. As a result, fetuses, valued for the future cotton they would pick or the price they would bring at auction, were bathed in the terror experienced by their mothers. However, it did not start there. The trauma of bone-altering physical labor and the ongoing torture of enslaved Black men was encoded in their bodies and transferred through the semen, which created the next generation. Thus, babies were conceived in trauma, incubated in trauma, then were born and experienced their own trauma that reinforced and confirmed what they had inherited genetically and what was being told to them, "Expect to be hurt. Protect yourself."

My parents were born roughly seventy years after the abolition of slavery, so the mental and genetic encoding was still fresh. To be clear, when slavery was abolished in 1865, the global economic system that promulgated was only an evolved version of the slavery system to include concepts like Jim Crow and sharecropping (and now the prison industrial complex and a plethora of other social, economic, and educational institutions that perpetuate oppressive conditions by design). Like babies born in slavery, my parents inherited the genetic code altered by trauma, observed the abuse and oppression endured by their caregivers, and experienced their own injustices throughout their lives. In 1955 when my parents were in their early 20s and late teens, the murder of Emmett Till made it painfully clear that there was still no safety for Blacks in Mississippi. My oldest sister was born a year later so of course soon after her birth, my parents migrated north to Toledo, Ohio. They were like many Black people in the southern states looking for a better, safer life. While in Ohio, they added to their family with my brother before moving on to Chicago and having two more girls (my sisters). They worked hard in a factory where many of their kin found stable jobs and built a life where their kids could live and enjoy experiences neither of them could when they were young. One important experience was family vacations. They worked hard to afford to take their family out of the city to enjoy life and be kids. In July 1968, they took a trip to a resort in Indiana full of families having fun with children playing and swimming in the onsite pond. My oldest sister Esther, who was thirteen at the time, was by the swimming pond. My brother Bobby (age twelve) was swimming, and my other sisters Felicia (age seven) and Lizette (age three), were with my parents back in their room getting ready to join Esther and Bobby at the pond. Esther was making friends with another girl who invited her to come check out her dolls or some cool toy. When she came back to the pool, she couldn't find Bobby and let my parents know. They looked for him to no avail and alerted the authorities that he was missing. The search led to the police dredging the pond with a crane. Eventually they hoisted my brother's body up out of the muck at the bottom of the pond by one leg as my parents and sister looked on. He had drowned. My family couldn't understand how a strong athletic twelve-year old boy, who knew how to swim, could drown surrounded by other adults and children. No one saw him struggle in the water. It was pronounced an accidental drowning, but my father suspected that Bobby was killed. You see it was 1968 in Indiana, a state where the Klu Klux Klan was known to be active (even though not in that area) and my family was the only Black family vacationing there. As a mother of two, I can't imagine the unspeakable pain of losing a child at all, let alone in that way. It is unbearable to think of seeing his lifeless body hoisted before them, like many of the lynchings of the old south. My parents experienced the same trauma as their ancestors had over a hundred years before. They left their home in Chicago just a few days prior, joyful and excited to vacation as a family seemingly living the American dream, only to return without one of their children, deeply wounded and in shock. My family, even my sisters, were devastated and in extreme grief, and blamed each other and themselves for not protecting him and being powerless to save him. This horrific, potentially racially motivated tragedy fortified the idea that had been passed down genetically, verbally, and through the observations of my parents as children in Mississippi—bad things will happen to you and your only power of protection is to try to expect and anticipate every scenario. Because it was a traumatic loss for the entire family, this idea of "expect the worse" became an impenetrable belief, not only in my parents' minds, but my sisters' as well.

My family did their best to move forward and deal with the loss of their only son and brother. My father's way of healing was to honor Bobby with two goals that he felt would accomplish this. One of his goals was to start businesses named after Bobby so that his name would light up a city block. In 1971, my parents opened Bobby's A-OK Grill, having purchased an established restaurant from a white man who was ready to retire. The clientele was all white since that part of Chicago's Southside had not yet fully browned. To keep the business alive, the seller and my father agreed that my father would work as the grill cook and learn the business, appearing as an employee, even though he was the owner. Just three years after losing his only son, my father immortalized Bobby's name. His 2nd goal was to have another son. He wanted a chance to protect his male child and groom him into manhood, an opportunity ripped from him just as Bobby was entering puberty. Thus, 1971 was a big year of redress for my father since it was also the year my mother became pregnant with their fifth child and he thought his second goal was manifesting. While my father was certain that his desire for another son was coming true, my mother secretly prayed she was having a girl. She shared this with me during one of her "cool of the evening" talks. She didn't want her son to have the pressure nor did she want the pain of what would seem like a "replacement" son. I also suspect she didn't want another Black male child that would be a target for racial violence. Her prayers were answered, and she gave birth to a baby girl, me. I was born December 23, 1971 during the transition from a universal year nine of endings and year one of new beginnings. I'm sure my father was somewhat disappointed, but he is a loving, committed father and didn't slight me in any way for being a girl, though he took me under his wing as a sort of imitation son. He chose to name me with Bobby's same initials, BCW following the path of his own initials RCW.

Growing up I often heard the story of how they were done having children, but chose to have me because they lost Bobby, so I was truly planned. As one might expect, I was an over-protected child. From birth to five-years old, I was pretty much only around relatives unless I was helping at our family business. Then at age five, I started kindergarten, terrified, and suddenly interacting with people not my family, with an ingrained sense of something bad about to happen. Two weeks later, the principal and my dad agreed that I was more advanced than the kindergarten class and I was moved to 1st grade. Another big shift occurred before I settled into the first transition and I shrunk even more. I didn't want to be seen or noticed for fear of attracting the "bad" thing waiting around the corner. I spent the next ten years learning how to armor up and protect myself from the impending doom. Unfortunately for my mental and physical health, that meant learning to analyze as many possible negative outcomes as I could and assess potential negative intentions from everyone. This equated to a habitual emotional state fluctuating between anxiety when ruminating about negative outcomes, and depression when assessing it all as a zero-sum game with no possible positive outcome. I was about fifteen when I thought I found the perfect combination of armor to avoid being hurt by bad things happening. I stopped caring; I stopped trying to live authentically; I stopped showing up as myself and stopped allowing myself to express my true thoughts and emotions. I heard the advice to "expect the worst" and prepare for it, but it seemed to me that my existence was the direct result of the worst that could happen to parents—losing a child.

By applying *The Work* outlined in Chapter 4, I am able to recognize the truth of how this proverb showed up in my life. My existence isn't a direct result of the worst possible situation, I am the direct result of love. My creation lay in the love my parents had for each other in their attempt to heal and recreate or redirect the love they still held for my brother. I am not the product of tragedy as I had internalized, I am the product of love. Love that was heavily laden with grief and sorrow, but still a pure, deeply radiating love. As a baby, I was a new life entering a household that was thick with depression and unresolved grief and sadness. Babies bring hope and soft emotions into a home. I have come to realize that my birth brought the hope that tomorrow can be better, and the pain of loss can become bearable. Now rather than "expect the worse" and be fearful of all the things that can go wrong in life, I expect the best and try to plan in a way to manifest the outcome I desire while leaving room for spirit to bless my life in unexpected ways.

"Fools names and fools faces are always seen in public places"

On face level, this phrase refers to graffiti taggers, both the authentic artists who express their creativity in public areas as well as the crude spray paint vandals who seek to deface public areas. This is another phrase Black folk transformed to be more relevant for the situation we were in. From slavery through Jim Crow, a Black person's safety often depended on keeping a low profile. Being noticed by white people could lead to becoming their target. As a woman, your body could be violated if the overseer or plantation owner took notice of you. As a man, you might be beaten or sold if you caught the eye of your enslavers – or worse if the mistress of the house took a fancy to you. Blacks were not allowed to look directly a white person, speak unless spoken to, or carry themselves in a way that indicated they were confident or thought they were equal to whites. Even the acceptable buffoonery of self-degrading acts for the entertainment of whites was foolish attention.

Back in the 80's on Chicago's Southside, it seemed that every viaduct or building side was covered in crude images, gang symbols, or some claim of territory. The more creative displays that beautified communities were few and far between. My parents were particularly vexed with this as owners of the building that housed our family business. The building was located next to a used car lot, which meant the entire side of the brick building was visible and accessible. From an advertising perspective, it was like owning a huge billboard with control over what messaging you wanted to share with thousands of by-passers. So, like the astute business people they were, they had the entire side of the building painted with advertising for our businesses. It would get worn over time, but I can remember it being refreshed a couple of times in my youth. My father would be so proud to see his son's name in big beautiful letters for everyone to see. Our family had three businesses operating out of one building with three separate storefronts—a restaurant, a barbershop, and a beauty supply that over the years would be changed to a takeout fried fish spot, then later, a takeout food and liquor store. Bobby's A-OK Grill, Bobby's Barbershop, Bobby's Beauty Supply, Bobby's Fish House, then Bobby's Liquor. As I mentioned, after my brother died, my father's way of coping was to immortalize his name as the brand for multiple businesses. These businesses, this building, and that outside wall with Bobby's name proudly on display and highly visible, was more than a source of income or method of advertising. They were life size altars to my brother. The fact that Bobby's name was in a public place but was not in the "fool" category was never a conflict in my mind. Since he died before I was born, it often seemed that his spirit was bigger than any earthly quibble.

Now imagine the frustration my parents felt when someone would graffiti tag their name on our building, particularly since the name or words spray-painted were often gang related or just vulgar nonsense. The emotional impact on my parents would be heavy and laden with the sadness of their loss of Bobby. Whenever this happened, my father would have to paint over it himself, which would remove the offensive tagging, but would still destroy the original design. Or they would begrudgingly pay someone to paint over the offense while maintaining the original aesthetic. Or, worst of all, they had to leave it for some time until they had the time or money to have it removed. Because of "fools" wanting to be "seen" in public places, my parents had to spend time and money to restore their monument to their deceased only son. This meant that every time a tagger decided to declare their existence by defacing our building, they brought to the surface, feelings of anger, rage, and grief in my parents.

Seeing and feeling those strong emotions from my parents intertwined with a seemingly mundane issue like graffiti became a bit twisted and truncated in my mind as a child. I was able to understand the basic lesson of respecting other people and their property. However, for me, the significance of "fool's names and fool's faces" was that being seen, allowing people to truly know me, brings pain. In the real-life situation, a stranger's decision to be "seen" in public via graffiti tagging caused my parents pain, grief, and anger. In the scenario I created internally and generalized across my life, I was both the perpetrator and the victim in that if I allow people to know me as I am, if I express myself authentically, if I am just me, people will think little of me, criticize me, and humiliate me. I learned as a child to suppress my expression and shrink in hopes of not being noticed, talked about, or picked on. I had my own translated versions of this proverb: "Keep your business out of the street," "Stay private, don't expose too much of yourself or you are a fool," and "Don't let people know you," or "It's foolish to be seen." I was particularly sensitive to being made fun of as a chubby girl. Navigating the, at times, cruel world of kids was hard since any attention would inevitably result in being called names, usually some variation of "fat." In high school, if I had the misfortune of having to run or jump in gym class, I would hear something like "earthquake!" followed or preceded by robust laughter. Or if I was bike riding with friends over the summer and wearing shorts, I'd hear "thunder thighs!" again preceded and/or followed by laughter. These types of experiences may have only happened a few times but became ingrained and strengthened my distorted fear of being seen and were critical components in my battle with depression. Turns out I'm not alone. A 2012 study found that Black women who internalized weight-related stigmatizing experiences are more likely to become depressed than white women, particularly if we avoid confronting the stigmatizing situations (Fettich, Chen 2012). How did I cope? I shrunk and retreated. I did less of the things that would bring attention to myself, which meant less physical activity, and less of the things I loved like music, art, and dance. I scanned people to determine what I needed to do or say to fit in and not be singled out. For years, if I heard a group of people laughing nearby, I would automatically assume they were laughing at me and feel a surge of anxiety.

Today, I perform on stage at festivals and events, dancing and singing with Afro-Brazilian or Afro-Cuban dance groups. I am the largest dancer on stage and sometimes I must get creative to make the costumes work. I am not triggered by people laughing nearby so I may not notice the laughter, or I'll just listen to absorb the positive energy emitted by the sound of joyful laughter. Where I used to be triggered to contract and hide within an exoskeleton, I now expand and flutter my wings without fear or shame. Getting to this point took several steps and many years and is work I continue today. The first step was gaining the self-awareness of how this "fools face" proverb was manifesting in my life. Fueling my effort to liberate myself was my decision to live fully and stop hiding.

"Being Black, you have to work twice as hard to get half as far"

Forever First Lady Michelle Obama said it to a group of graduating Tuskegee University students. Papa Pope said it to Olivia in season three, episode one of *Scandal*. Black parents have drilled it into the minds of their children for decades—ever since the possibility of mainstream achievement seemed within reach. This "Plantation Proverb" speaks to the reality that as descendants of the enslaved, we are still subjected to political, social, educational, financial, environmental, judicial and healthcare institutions that systemically subjugate, marginalize, and target us, to weigh down our progress and ascension, so that the dominating 1% can maintain control over the masses. Racism and oppression have slowed the progress of Black and Brown people and many poor white people have lost their own humanity by believing in the false reality that despite how destitute they may be, their access to white privilege elevates their worth.

White kids are told they can be anything they want to be, and they are told directly or subconsciously that it's their white privilege that affords them this gift of limitless potential. Then there are the many white people who are unaware or are in denial that they are automatically granted advantage based on the color of their skin. Meanwhile, Black kids are told to work hard and when you think you are doing enough to achieve your goals, double up and work twice as hard because you don't have white privilege on your side. For some Black kids' life is already so hard with every institution stacked against you, that it's near impossible to stay focused and on track towards an education or career. Then we are told to work harder. In short, stress starts to build up early in a Black child's mind, body, and life.

The presence and effects of stress on Black children has been proven. In the Philadelphia ACE Study, a collaborative project led by the Institute for Safe Families, it was found that children exposed to racism have worse health, struggle with concentration, and have higher risks of anxiety and depression. In fact, exposure to racism is compounded when Black parents—fictitious like Papa Pope, real life like my parents, or world famous like the First Lady Michelle Obama—teach children that being Black means a life of working harder and striving to be smarter for only a partial reward simply because they lack white privilege. I believe that simply being Black in America, or in the world for that matter, means being exposed to racism. Therefore, the physical, emotional, and mental health of all Black people are negatively affected starting in childhood.

Let's take a walk through my own life with this thought of "working twice as hard."

Growing up on the Southside of Chicago, I attended the neighborhood elementary school and was always one of the top students in my class. By 4th grade, I had participated in several summer programs for gifted kids throughout the city and been moved to different grade levels at my neighborhood school to keep me intellectually challenged. The next year I was part of an effort to bring the city's gifted students together, into a new school, and an advanced program. I was bussed out of my neighborhood along with kids from all over the city. For the first time other than in brief summer programs, I was in class with white, Latino, and Asian kids. And they were ALL smart! I wasn't the only Black kid, but I was hyper aware of any differences between the white kids and me. All I could think is how I had to be smarter, but it would never be enough. These thoughts would cycle through my mind at speeds too fast to articulate or rationalize. They just became background noise that contributed to an emotional undertone of anxiety in my life. It didn't take long before I had my first anxiety attack. I was in 5th grade. I remember the rapid pace of my breath and heart beat while feeling overwhelming panic—and I was at home just thinking about going to school the next day. "I'm scared! I'm not smart enough! Everybody is smart at this school," I thought. I attempted to cope with the constant anxiety by burying my fear in emotional eating. This is when lifelong habits started to form that would impair my nervous system and create cortisol spikes, the stress hormone that leads to hypertension, depression, anxiety, and obesity not to mention weakened immune systems, diabetes, and osteoporosis.

By the time I made it to 7th grade, I was a moody, semi depressed pre-teen who struggled with low self-worth and fear. My anxiety and fears about my intellectual inferiority, infected my psyche, replicating itself until I could not distinguish between those lies and my truth. This "infection" was continuing to manifest itself in my body; it had already dominated my sympathetic nervous system, keeping my heart rate and blood pressure constantly elevated, slowing down my digestion resulting in frequent constipation, and relaxing my bladder as I wet the bed until about nine or ten years old. Then at eleven years old, I was in 7th grade, but I was in high school. This gifted program included 7th and 8th grade students attending class in a high school with a separate homeroom, but some classes integrated with freshmen students. I was terrified every day. The social awkwardness that would be natural for a 7th grader, was intensified by being a year younger than nearly everyone else in my grade, further amplified by sharing classes with fourteen-year-old kids and passing in the hall with fellow students as old as eighteen. The stress and anxiety were wreaking havoc on my immune system. Every cold or flu bug that went by, I caught it. Looking back, I see that when the stress would be too much to carry, I would drop into a depression or breakdown and get sick. Missing a week or two of school back then, due to illness or injury, was common.

The emotional/mental "infection" took another turn in college and my adult years, with frequent severe migraines. These episodes of extreme inflammation would take me out for at least 24 hours and be full blown with light and noise sensitivity and sometimes vomiting. Later when I had become a wife, mother of two, and a stressed professional, I would learn to work through the migraines when they hit on a weekday. I would spend most weekends at home with an ice mask, in a dark room, while my husband kept the kids busy. I was not only experiencing the stress effects of having to "work twice as hard" as a kid, but every milestone from high school, to college, and in my career increased the stakes. Now, keeping up impacted my livelihood, promotions, and ability to earn a fair salary compared to my white peers—particularly white men. The older I got, the more obvious the advantage white men and women had over other groups. I discovered the corporate hierarchy that placed Black men and women near or at the bottom, regardless of education, intelligence, or actual job performance. I found myself angry that I worked my ass off to learn more and excel at my job but would see mediocracy rewarded with promotions or executive sponsorship. This frequently happened among white men. They were gifted at speaking up in a meeting, at the right time, in front of the right people, to help their career. Rarely were their contributions particularly insightful; often it was just a repackaging of something someone else had already said. Then I noticed that white women formed their own support systems, watching out for each other and ensuring when one or two of them were promoted, they would look out for their "clique," who were often neighbors or weekend/happy hour hang out buddies. I wanted to succeed, so not only was it expected that I work harder and be smarter, I also had to analyze my peers, build alliances, and spend time away from my family to build work relationships after a long workday. It pissed me off, yet I feared failing. I feared my family not being able to have a variety of life experiences. I feared my kids feeling ashamed because we were not wealthy like a lot of their friends and families in the Pacific Northwest. I feared losing the race to success. I feared not being enough. I feared those white men and women who were able to benefit from their white privilege. I feared breaking under the weight of often being the sole representation of Black culture in my corporate environment with the self-appointed task of demonstrating the brilliance of all Black people. I feared so much that I was deeply angry and overly anxious. It was during this time that my blood pressure became noticeable. It started as pre-hypertension, but I avoided medication for a couple years because I didn't like how it made me feel or the idea of being dependent on pharmaceuticals. The impact of my blood pressure spikes and migraines would interchange until the pain would send me to urgent care. I'd take a few days to feel better and recoup then be back at the grind, working until 3am and oscillating between depression and anxiety.

I have known for many years that we live in a society that has erected barriers specifically aimed at impeding the economic progress of Black and Brown people. However, it took the techniques outlined in Chapter 4 for me to internalize that I don't have to function with the thought of competition. I can do my best, take care of myself and my family, and have a joyous life. Maybe that means I don't get promoted as often as my white peers or make as much money as them until we have eradicated institutional racism and gender inequality. Maybe that means I take my brain power out of corporate America and put it to use for my own business or my community. Maybe I define what success is beyond the purely economic definition given by the very oppressors who designed the system in their favor. Perhaps I realize that we are playing a long game and my success has already been paid for by the blood, sweat, and tears of my ancestors. Yeah, definitely that.

CHAPTER 3

Mammies and Jezebels:
When Enslavers Define You

The multi-generational advice given to me through "Plantation Proverbs" was not the only contributor to my core belief of "Fat, Black, and Unlovable." As the primary interpreter of American life, television is a major factor in shaping Black youths' perception of reality (i.e., how people treat each other) into social reality (i.e., how we interact with peers). According to a study by communications researchers, Tan and Tan, Black children of my generation watched 16% more television than white kids. Like many other Black teens, by the time I was 18, I watched about 25,000 hours of television compared to spending just 11,000 hours in school. Furthermore, there was a growing concern among parents and educators that excessive TV viewing would: 1) influence a Black child's attitude toward his or her own racial group; 2) the lack of or demeaning representation of Blacks on television would foster low self-concepts; and 3) teach values contradictory to what was taught in the home. Moreover, the National Opinion Research Center conducted a study finding that Blacks had more confidence in the validity of television programming than whites. In fact, in their article published in The Black Scholar, researchers Robert Staples and Terry Jones cite a study conducted by Tony Brown, producer and host of *Tony Brown's Journal*, a Black public affairs PBS program. Brown's study found that 1) Blacks prefer programs which feature Blacks; 2) Blacks perceive television as representative of real life more than whites; and 3) Black adolescents are more likely to use television to learn how to behave with the opposite sex. Lastly, researchers found a correlation between high television exposure and low self-esteem among Blacks, but no such causal relationship exists among whites.

These facts beg the question: How were Black people represented in media? Prior to the inception of television, most characters representing Black people in Vaudeville shows were played by white actors in black face. Once television programing was introduced in the 1940's, Black people were portrayed as non-threatening and subservient characters. Following the height of the civil rights era in the 1960s, Blacks appeared in 46% of all TV programs during a one-week period in 1970, but by 1973 we appeared with less frequency and in lower status occupations. (Staples, 1985) Researchers, Greenberg and Baptiste-Fernandez conducted a content analysis study of primetime shows from 1975-1978. They found that there were very few Blacks characters and those that were represented, were more likely to be poor, jobless, or in low-status occupations. Furthermore, Black women were not in prominent roles and were portrayed as dependent, submissive, and less intelligent. This quality and quantity of Black representation on television continued into the 1980s with 49% of Blacks on televisions in roles as criminals, servants, entertainers, or athletes.

It would appear to me that the media industry schemed to diminish the Black community, leaving many of us with a belief that we could never be successful, happy, or fulfilled. The diabolical socialization efforts of using media to teach adverse attitudes and behaviors as well as self-concepts and social roles, contributed significantly to the texture and strength of "Fat, Black, and Unlovable." The endeavors of the media industry significantly contributed to this belief that has impacted my world view, stress response, and ultimately my health and longevity. What follows below is an historical analysis of how Black women have been presented in media, told through the lens of stereotypes, and their impact on me.

You Betta Look Like Bunny Debarge!

I am a Black woman. When I was a teenager, I was a Black girl searching for a way to find my place in the world despite the shame I felt, yet did not understand, and could not articulate. I was desperate for a benchmark to define my beauty, to assess it, to rate it. The human ego often seeks to define itself through comparison to others. My ego knew I was a Black woman, but it struggled to know what that meant and determine if it was good or bad—if *I* was inherently good or bad. Was I beautiful? Can a Black woman *be* beautiful? Was I desirable? Does *anyone* desire a Black woman? Everything around me said that the standard of beauty consisted of European features, from skin, hair, eye color, and especially hair texture. The message hammered into Black women was and still is "since you're not a white woman, in order to be considered beautiful, you better have few or no African features." The standard for a pretty, Black girl back then was long straight hair and light skin. A great example of "light is right" was the musical group and family, *DeBarge*. Popular in the 80s with my favorite hits like *"All This Love," "I Like It,"* and *"Time Will Reveal,"* DeBarge was a group of four brothers and one sister with talent compared to the *Jackson Five*. The lead singer, El DeBarge, became what made Black girls swoon and the only female in the group, his sister, Bunny DeBarge, was the prototype of what Black teen boys desired. But Bunny isn't the only example from that period, I reference her because any Black person alive in the 80s will know what I'm talking about, and others can do a web search. A quick scan of music videos, movies, and TV shows of the 80s will show clearly that the only Black women who were considered beautiful or admirable were those whose dominant features were European.

Why were Black women only represented in this way? Two main factors in my opinion, projected and internalized racism. It is no secret that the entertainment industry was dominated by white men with the power and means to decide who gets record or movie deals to manifest their artistic vision or who were selected to simply churn out content that the studio or label deemed as "urban." And when artists managed to produce work that reflected their "Africanness" it was still the white male executives that owned the means of production. Thus, they made the decision on who was marketed and presented to the world and whose projects were shelved, never to see the light of day. That's not to say that Black artists in the 80s were not talented or worthy of their success, but we will never know what they would have produced or how they would have presented themselves without the coercion of a systemically racist media and entertainment industry. We will also never know what talented journalists, filmmakers, screen writers, actresses/actors, musicians, or singers the world could have been gifted with were it not for systemic racism in media production and distribution industries. Entire generations have been influenced by the actions of business decision makers acting out their own biases and prejudices. As a result, women representing beauty in entertainment during the 80s did not look like me and the message I received was clear. There was a hierarchy to beauty and femininity in this world and I was at the bottom of it.

As a response to the trauma of racism, some of our people reject entertainment or media that reflect expressions of our Blackness, choosing to divorce themselves from the part of us that makes us Black—the African in us. We know that trauma is passed through generations via epigenetics and the DNA expression resulting from the trauma of slavery is reinforced by contemporary racism. The concept of colorism—internalized racism based on skin color—is an unspoken "Plantation Proverb" stemming from lighter skinned enslaved people receiving better treatment from overseers and plantation owners than those with darker skin. Psychologically, pain and suffering were associated with darker skin and an informal caste system evolved. That wound still exists in the Black community today and was even more prevalent in the 80's. Internalized racism can manifest as self-hatred towards that part of ourselves, our color and ethnicity, that seemed to bring our families pain and shame due to slavery, colonization, racism, and discrimination.

This self-hatred has been studied. In the 1940's, psychologists Kenneth and Mamie Clark conducted the famous "Doll Test" to measure how segregation affected Black children. The study, which demonstrated the damaging effects of segregation, helped in the 1954 Brown v Board of Education case, leading to the desegregation of U.S. schools. The researchers asked Black children to choose between a white doll and a black doll with a series of questions and found that the children overwhelmingly preferred white over Black. Most dark or medium brown children in the study were able to identify themselves correctly (73% and 81% respectively), choosing the Black doll as looking like them, while only 20% of light complexioned children identified with the black doll. On a surface level, this makes sense, the browner a child's skin was, the more they identified with the Black doll. The issue is that not only did most children prefer to play with the white doll, they did so because they viewed the white doll as nice, pretty, or good and the brown doll as mean, ugly, or bad. One doesn't have to be a mathematician to compute, Black children saw *themselves* as ugly or bad.

Fast forward sixty years later, past the 80's when I grew up, to 2005. Kira Davis was a young Black female film student in Harlem, who decided her film project would examine issues of beauty and "blackness" among teen women. In her 7-min documentary, *A Girl Like Me*, Davis demonstrates the limitations that society places on beauty as it relates to skin color and hair texture. Furthermore, she replicated Clarks' doll test with preschoolers from a Harlem daycare. 15 of the 21 children interviewed preferred the white doll. It was particularly painful to see one girl choose the Black doll when asked which doll was bad, her reason being because it was Black. Then when asked which doll looks like her, she hesitates, then shamefully pushes the Black doll forward. Sixty years after desegregation and Black children still saw themselves as bad and unattractive because of their darker skin.

In 2009, the producers of Good Morning America wanted to see how things had changed since the original Clark study given that we had recently elected our first Black president. While their results indicated that things had improved some, the impact on Black girls was still daunting. 47 percent of the Black girls in the study said the white doll was prettier. This was clearly an issue of self-image specific to the experience of being a Black girl in this society. Furthermore, in 2010 CNN hired Margaret Beale Spencer, a University of Chicago professor and leading child development researcher, as a consultant to design and execute a pilot study like the famous Clark study. While her research did not produce definitive conclusions on children and race, it clearly indicated that "we are still living in a society where dark things are devalued, and white things are valued," said Spencer.

I am not a white woman. My skin is best described as milk chocolate, distinctively brown with a tendency to evolve to dark chocolate in summer months like a 70% cacao delicacy. Even though in the distant past I have donned grey or hazel contact lenses, my natural eye color is dark brown or black as is my hair unless I chose some other fun color. My hair grows in tight coils and could be referred to as "nappy" or "kinky." My lips are full and command attention whether they are bare, dry and chatting away or sparkling, glossy and tightly closed in silence. To some, my nose may resemble a mix of Indigenous, European, and African ancestry, but still would not cause confusion about my ethnic identity. My nose reminds me that there is at least one white man in my bloodline—a plantation and slave owner in Mississippi—who helped himself to the body of one of my Ancestral Mothers. My 3rd great grandmother, "Black Sara," was an enslaved African and my 3rd great grandfather, Master Granberry was the plantation owner. Sara bore him several children and the laws in this country at the time meant that he owned this little family he created and could do whatever he pleased to her and their children. I wonder what trauma she experienced, and I have inherited? Did she have any choice in with whom she lay and had children? Was she even allowed to raise them, mother them, nurture them? How many of my Ancestral Mothers were raped by their enslavers, saw their mate mutilated and lynched, or had their children ripped from their breast to be sold away and never seen again. My cousin has been able to trace this part of our maternal lineage because much of the bloodline remained fixed in one location. My mother was raised on the same plot of land that was part of the plantation upon which Black Sara was enslaved. There is a pain inherent in being a Black woman that is old and embedded in our DNA. I can feel the pain of my ancestors and perhaps my past life that suffered humiliation, powerlessness, and violation. I can feel their pain and suffering, but I also feel the ancient strength of my Ancestral Mothers. I feel how they survived to proliferate the bloodline despite the atrocities around them.

No, I was not a white girl or woman. I still am not. I did not look like Bunny DeBarge. I still don't. I am a Black Woman. For all my teen years and most of my adult life, I didn't know how to define myself as a Black woman in this world; if I was good, pretty, or desirable; if a Black woman could ever be considered good, pretty, or desirable. I would hold these uncertainties in my heart along with the wounds of ancestral enslavement until my heart could hold it no more.

Gimme a Break! Mammy of the 80's

The standard of beauty was established in my mind as a thin white woman with blue eyes and long flowing hair, which I clearly was not. Thus, I continued my search for where I fit into the American beauty and worthiness landscape. Like most Black folks back in the 80s, I gravitated to the few and far between TV shows that featured a Black character. One of my favorite shows was *Gimme a Break!* starring Nell Carter. I watched the show religiously along with *Good Times, The Jefferson's, Sanford and Son, Benson,* and even the *A-Team.* I can attest to the fact that finally seeing myself reflected on television was exciting – at first. However, the more I watched *Gimme a Break!,* the more I resented my body, my skin, and the very idea that I identified with this character. As Tony Brown's study revealed about Black people, I perceived television as representative of real life and how I could expect to interact with boys. I hated the thought that my life could one day resemble this character's life in any way. *Gimme a Break!* was simply the more recent segment of this country's attack on Black women's self-esteem using a 100-year-old strategy with modern techniques.

Let's take a step back to the 1800's when white men created "Mammy," a persona of a de-sexualized Black woman diligently, faithfully, and subserviently caring for a white family as her own. The original concept was propaganda created during slavery to support the lie that enslaved Africans preferred to be slaves and the institution of slavery was an act of mercy. This caricature attempted to paint the false picture that Mammy was a loved member of the white family, but truly, the family owned her. Unlike Sambo who was a lazy schemer (the Black male caricature fabricated by white plantation owners to support slavery), Mammy could be trusted to the upmost. She would be sure to tend to her "master's" house and possessions better than her own, befriend his wife, be her confidant and protector when needed, and serve his children until her dying breath. Mammy's world consisted only of nurturing her white family and going to church, sacrificing her own needs in favor of the needs of her white family. She was depicted as an older dark-skinned Black woman who was morbidly obese with a very shiny face and her hair wrapped in a scarf. Though she had extremely large breasts, they were contained and covered in a way that resembled comfortable pillows rather than female anatomy. By extracting all sexual or sensual qualities from the myth of Mammy, white men created reasonable doubt in the public's mind to refute the well-known and accurate truth that they sexually abused the African women they enslaved. "A white man sexually attracted to Mammy? That's ridiculous!!" During this time before rape was understood as a violent act of power and control rather than sexual gratification, the false idea perpetuated by the Mammy myth was that a white man would not choose Mammy over his idealized white wife.

Once plantation owners created Mammy and effectively spread the propaganda, she started to show up in popular culture such as Aunt Chloe in Uncle Tom's Cabin (Stowe, 1852). After slavery was abolished, Mammy continued to gain traction through the Jim Crow era. From *The Birth of a Nation* (Griffith, 1915) or the first talking movie *The Jazz Singer* (Crosland, 1927) with Al Jolson in blackface singing "Mammy," to Aunt Delilah in *Imitation of Life* (Laemmle & Stahl, 1934). In fact, *Imitation of Life* was remade in 1959 (Hunter & Sirk) earning the actress in the Mammy role, Juanita Moore, an Academy Award nomination. But, the first Black actress to actually win an Academy Award was Hattie McDaniel twenty years earlier for her Mammy role as Scarlett O'Hara's sassy, but loyal servant in *Gone with The Wind* (Selznick & Fleming, 1939). In 1950, Mammy even found her way to the small screen when ABC was the first network to present a television show featuring a Black actress. Ethel Waters portrayed the dedicated maid of a white family in *Beulah* on ABC from 1950 to 1953.

Right along with media and entertainment, the growing advertising industry further perpetuated the Mammy myth using the image as a branding tool to sell a variety of household products such as Aunt Sally Baking Soda, Luzianne Coffee, Aunt Dinah Molasses, and Fun-To-Wash Detergent as well as other sewing and cleaning supplies. The most famous and enduring Mammy persona is Aunt Jemima. In 1889, the name was borrowed from a song in a Mammy skit performed by a minstrel group and used to promote a new self-rising flour. Nancy Green, born a slave in 1834, was used to impersonate Aunt Jemima for over 30 years until her death on September 23, 1923. She made appearances all over the country, cooking and serving pancakes while singing songs and telling stories of the "good ol' south." The branding strategy was successful and expanded to include premium giveaways like dolls and dishware, further spreading the Aunt Jemima Mammy image. The R.T. Davis Mill Company which owned the product and brand, was renamed the Aunt Jemima Mills Company in 1914, and had become so successful that the Quaker Oats Company purchased it in 1926. Quaker Oats continued to promote the Aunt Jemima product line with live Mammy impersonators. It wasn't until 1989, 100 years after the creation of the Aunt Jemima brand, that Quaker Oats dropped the Jim Crow-era stereotype and modernized the Mammy image to the branding still in use today.

In 1981, NBC aired *Gimme a Break!* during prime-time to millions of Americans, presenting the character, Nellie Ruth Harper, as a new version of Mammy. The show, along with the character, was created by Seattle native and former writer for Bob Hope, Mort Lachman, and Sy Rosen, a well-known Hollywood TV writer and producer. This story about a Black woman was written by two white men just as the original Mammy concept was created by white plantation owners. These two white men created a story where the Black female main character agrees to give up her own hopes and dreams as a professional singer to be the housekeeper and nanny for the police chief and his three daughters. Much like the original Mammy concept, the character happily sacrificed her life goals to dedicate herself to her white family, supposedly out of mutual love.

Over the years of the show, Nell had boyfriends that came and went, a deadbeat ex-husband, and girlfriends with varying degrees of intelligence, but the overall focus of this character's life was caring for this family. After a couple of seasons, an additional child was added to the show in the form of a foster son, who Nell also cared for. By the time the show ended, the chief had died, the girls were grown, and Nell had moved across the country to care for the foster son and his younger brother. The writers made this story transition with Nell visiting from California to check on the boys, now living in New York with their unstable father. However, she is forced to stay there permanently when the deceased chief's father sells the Kanisky family home, leaving her essentially homeless. So much for being a beloved member of the family. Her dedication to this family knew no bounds, much like the fictitious Mammy, but she had no property rights and she was booted out.

When I was a kid and wanted something from my mother, I liked to say "Mama" over and over in different ways. Usually, it would annoy her just enough to break through the mental barriers she had up to tune out the unnecessary chatter that kids sometimes spout. Occasionally I went too far in my "mama" variations and slipped into forbidden territory and called her "Mammy." It pierced through her blockade and grabbed her attention quicker and more completely than any other of my creative "mama" variations. She snapped to attention and sternly said "Don't call me that!" She was clearly both offended and angry, not at me, but at the existence of the term itself. When I asked why, she explained that it was something racists called Black women in the south where she grew up. I don't remember her offering much more explanation than that. She had similar reactions to Mammy figurines and trinkets in gas stations during our road trips to Mississippi. She wanted no part of Mammy. The image and concept of Mammy evoked a pain in her that seemed historical, possibly an unspoken "Plantation Proverb" to reject this fictitious identity.

Even still, I had no idea why as I watched *Gimme A Break!* my self-disgust grew. I didn't have the tools to critically evaluate what I was seeing or to correlate what I was feeling to my mother's pain about Mammy. I just knew the show's main character was heavy set, brown skinned, and one of the few personifications on TV in which I could see myself. But this character wasn't admired or desired which meant that I would not be either. She didn't have a husband and family of her own, so in my mind it meant that it wasn't likely that I ever would either. There was no image of a man that loved and desired her unconditionally just as she was so what hope did I have to experience this kind of love, given that she was me (in my mind)? Her place in the world was ultimately to serve her white family. Her needs, aspirations, and desires didn't matter and to me it seemed that none of mine mattered in the world either. That's just the way it was for fat Black women – destined to be unlovable. In many ways, "Fat, Black, and Unlovable" is a description of Mammy. But, as much as I internalized this Mammy image, there was still a feeling inside me that I was more than that. I was more than what the idiot box (my mother's name for the TV) told me I was. I tucked away my identity as Mammy hoping no one else saw her in me while I searched for a version of me that could replace her.

Video ho's — Jezebels Need Love Too

In my late teens and early twenties, I was still on a hunt for external validation to define myself. What other paths seemed open to a young Black woman desperately searching to feel worthy of love, but didn't know that love is a state of being within oneself? I was a young woman whose flawed thinking reasoned that the degree to which she was worthy of love would be evidenced by the degree to which she received what seemed like love from others. What young Black woman could I emulate that seemed to get the attention and notoriety that many young women like me craved, but couldn't seem to inspire or maintain? There were times that I wished I was of mixed race, but I didn't have European features and wasn't considered beautiful by popular standards, so partaking of the "Bunny DeBarge" advantage was out. The closest reflection of myself I saw in media was Nell Carter in a Mammy role, but I worked hard to hide that shameful correlation. I couldn't stand seeing myself as a selfless sexless caretaker without needs, a man, or a family of my own, and I certainly didn't want others to see me that way. You know which Black women seemed to have it all back in the late 80s and early 90s from my flawed mind's perspective? A Black woman who was never lonely or broke, always pampered and in control (or so I thought). What woman appeared to be admired, desired, and sought after? The modern-day Jezebel aka the "Video Ho" of the 90's (or I should say "video vixen" to be politically correct)!

First, let's discuss a little history to understand the depth and archaism of this issue for Black women. The "Jezebel" caricature of Black women as hyper-sexual, immoral, and promiscuous, predates the Mammy stereotype. This fictitious Black woman was created by European colonists invading Africa with their Anglo-Saxon and Puritan values, judging indigenous tribes and their native customs of dress, celebrations, and relationships as immoral. This view of Black women as hedonistic savages was created by slave traders as another justification for slavery and excuse for the horrific sexual abuse of Black women. Slave masters or overseers violently raped enslaved female Africans or coerced them to pretend to want sex with white men by threat of beatings, death of loved ones, or seeing their children sold. Slave owners also assigned enslaved girls and women to their sons and relatives as coming of age gifts or prostituted them for financial gain. If the stereotype of Mammy sent the message that no white man would want to have sex with a Black woman, then Jezebel portraying Black women as lewd sexual predators, enabled white men to feign helplessness to the advances of the "hot Black bitch." Once the slave trade was illegal and U.S. slavers were no longer able to import men, women, and children directly from Africa, breeding slaves within the existing slave population became a critical strategy for continuing to grow America's wealth. This meant that slave owners had even more at stake with the falsehood of the lustful and fertile Black woman (combined with sexual stereotypes of Black men which were equally damaging). The Jezebel concept not only gave white men moral permission to rape and sexually abuse Black women and girls, but also supported the notion of the economic necessity of breeding human slaves. Every distorted image placed upon Black women had its counterpart for Black men, like in this case, the big stud seeking sex at every turn, usually with white women if given a chance. This was also important to the United States' economic system of breeding slaves as they picked the biggest and strongest enslaved African men to impregnate enslaved women. A Black woman's body was not her own; it was loaned out, pimped out, poked and prodded, stripped and beaten, given away, sold away, and devalued while our wombs used to build a nation and our breasts to nourish all children, even those children that we would call "mass'ah."

Yeah, the history is pretty fucked up and one of the saddest parts is that it didn't end in 1865 with slavery. Through the Jim Crow era, Mammy was the most prevalent caricature of Black women, but Jezebel was vastly disseminated as well. She was depicted as a half-naked or fully naked, sometimes pregnant Black woman or girl on souvenir and novelty items. Then Jezebel resurged in the Blaxploitation films of the 70s and the personification lives on in films today.

I grew up in the age of the "video ho" aka "video vixen" aka "model" aka "dancer". These were beautiful women with bodies well-endowed with breasts, butts, and hips that became the mainstay in music videos in the 90s, particularly rap videos. Usually clad in lingerie or bikinis, these women could be found not only in rap videos "poppin' that p*ssy" or being "rump shakers," but also in magazines and at parties as eye candy or a twisted version of a party favor. But this time it wasn't just white men objectifying and over-sexualizing Black women, it was our own Black men as well, to sell more albums and enhance their image. Don't get me wrong, this is not an indictment of rap of any period or region (though I am super selective with current music calling itself hip hop). I came of age along with hip-hop, grew up in Chi-town, went to college in the "dirty south" and shared a house with a few NOCAL sistas (northern California, Bay Area), lived in Jersey, and married a true New Yorker so my musical palate is inherently hip-hop based and knows no geographical bounds. But, clearly, the decades and generations of stereotypical images have been internalized among Black men as well as Black women. Projected racism was a factor as well since decision makers such as record label executives, video directors, and casting directors were typically white men despite the Black artists and target audience.

It is embarrassing to realize I thought being like a video vixen was a viable way to be loved. Part of me is disgusted by some of the lyrics and objectified depictions of women in general. I have always loved to dance and some of my favorite music back in the day (besides house music, I am from Chicago after all), was Miami bass music from groups like the *Too Live Crew*. If you are not familiar, this group was known for controversial near pornographic lyrics and music videos with hits such as *Me so Horny* and *Pop that P*ssy*. I can recall getting my dance on to these cuts while wishing I had a body "worthy" of being one of the bikini or lingerie clad ladies in the music video. In my mind, looking like a video vixen would mean I was worthy of being desired. But I must admit my interest in this group died quickly as the words and depiction of women felt grimy—sort of like auditory rape, if that could be a thing. Then there was the west coast sound with rappers such as Too Short, DJ Quik, and AMG. These rappers' music was also quite danceable with banging beats and sexual lyrics that were often demeaning to women. They each had their own rap style, but the consistency across all their videos was shapely, fit, young women with small waists, flat stomachs, large breasts and "clappable' asses in string bikinis or "Daisy Dukes" shorts. The feminist in me is ashamed that I ever listened or danced to this music and saddened that I ever wanted to be the target of the objectification. But the reality is that I craved love so badly that I would have accepted it in this form.

While I remember dancing to these west coast artists and others, there is one artist, song, and video that really impacted me—Tupac's *I Get Around*. Unlike other artists, I thought Tupac was attractive and incredibly gifted, but carried a lot of anger. He was unpredictable in that you never knew if his music would be thought-provoking social commentary, an angry tirade towards another rapper, or a party song where sex and pretty girls were the entertainment. *I Get Around* was a great party song with a smooth beat and lyrical flow that was funny and light-hearted compared to most of the rap music at the time. The video stuck to the formula of bikinis and sexy women. However, two of the women in the video were heavier with darker skin than the other ladies. These two women chased Tupac much to his dismay/chagrin/disgust—pick a word. The women were older so it's not clear if they were supposed to be someone's mother or just party crashers. Unfortunately, as much as I wanted to look like the other women in the video, I identified with the two heavier, darker women that no one wanted. The message my mind latched on to was unless my body looked like the video girls hanging by the pool, I would always chase love, but never obtain it.

Over time, the exploitation of Black women seems to have diminished as many female artists have taken control of their branding. Talented women are embracing their sexuality, leveraging it, and creating a brand around it that they own. Consider Beyoncé or Jill Scott. Many women of color in the music industry are now using their sexuality to express their own creativity or benefit their own careers as entertainers rather than using their bodies or looks to get attention from men or help men sell more records. It is inspiring to see female artists today start to reclaim our sexual empowerment.

Energized by growing examples of empowered feminine sexuality, I began to do the work outlined in Chapter 4 to change my thinking about my own body. A sexy body isn't about attracting lasting love or a faithful mate, those things can be experienced regardless of what you look like and isn't guaranteed to anyone. My body and my sexuality are simply extensions of who I am. Quite frankly, a strong sexy body means different things to different people. In fact, the more I accept my body as it is, with stretch marks and jiggly thighs, the sexier and more empowered I feel. The more I do *The Work*, the more I develop a deeper intimacy with myself that allows me to open to the love within me and share that love with others. This work helps me inhabit my body more completely to feel sensual pleasure throughout life, not just during sex. The tools I have gathered are helping me reconnect with my soul and remember who I am. I learned that what attracts a mate, inspires romantic love, and creates desire, originates beyond the earthly trappings of a fit body. Sensuality, sexuality, and desire originate from your soul, the essence of who you are and draws to it its likeness. I also learned that sexuality is integral to existence as it is the catalyst for the creation of life. Sexuality can attract people to one another to procreate as well as attract particles to combine and create matter—another aspect of Oṣùn's energy. The problem is that the divine flame of love that was within me, got smothered in beliefs like "Fat, Black, and Unlovable". My mind said, "Ok, that's what I am," despite my shame of and aversion to this belief. As my vision narrowed to only see and think that which aligned to this belief, my actions and reactions were based on this false reality. It was always frustrating to want this perfect body, so I could finally be loved. Yet, I could not achieve it because I didn't love myself enough to nourish, hydrate, rest, and exercise my body properly, not to mention the vicious habit of emotional eating to numb my sadness and shame. I suppressed my identification with Mammy and being a Jezebel felt unobtainable.

Little did I know they would combine and morph into the next identity I would emotionally claim.

Welfare Queens and Strong Single Mothers — Two Sides of One Coin

By now I'm in my early twenties and coming out of the misguided desire for the attention of a video vixen. I never consciously made the choice to try on these personas, but I can see where my search for self-acceptance took me down these paths and these next Black woman stereotypes were no different. They are two separate, but interrelated stereotypes, the Strong Single Mother and the Welfare Queen, both usually depicted as single Black mothers raising multiple children by multiple absent fathers. Neither has ever been married or had a solid supportive romantic relationship. Both have endured infidelity and relationship drama and seem to choose men only to fulfill physical needs or out of loneliness. Both love their children, but how they demonstrate their love may differ based on how more or less healed they are from their own childhood. Neither woman may have a balanced view of what self-love and self-care are, resulting in either over indulgence of numbing agents (food, smoking, drugs, sex, etc) and/or complete neglect of self. Because the children came early in their lives, these women are usually under educated with limited opportunities for significant employment. There are only a few things that distinguish these women from each other—the source of their income, how society judges them, and how they judge themselves.

In 1995, I became a Welfare Queen, a myth created by former U.S. President Ronald Reagan and perpetuated in American media in the 60s through 80s. Reagan painted a picture of a welfare mother that defrauded the government and the American taxpayers by lying to receive welfare benefits they did not deserve. From there, stories in the media about poverty became synonymous with images of Black women and their children. It wasn't long before America bought the false idea that welfare rolls were filled with Black mothers avoiding employment by having children to get government checks. This stereotype carries Jezebel qualities since she is perceived as being morally lose and promiscuous with many children and fathers. In the eyes of hypocritical America, it is the government that provided for the children much like the slave master provided for Mammy 100 years prior. Not only is it a lie that most welfare recipients are Black women, this judgement ignores the many historical and systemic issues that created the circumstances that would lead to single parent households and economic disparity. Nevertheless, this Welfare Queen persona spread much like its predecessors Mammy and Jezebel, but this time more easily convincing Black women to define themselves by this false character.

However, I digress; yes in 1995, I became a Welfare Queen. Despite my struggles with depression, I was attending college in Atlanta. I shared a house with two friends and had spurts of enjoying life, alternating with episodes of major depression. My on/off-again boyfriend of six years had moved to Atlanta from our hometown of Chicago and we continued to be on and off periodically. One day I had a doctor appointment at a clinic near campus that offered a sliding fee scale for students. I was there to get a routine gynecologist checkup and inquire about mild pelvic pains I was having sporadically. I went through all the usual intake processes: weight, height, blood, urine, blood pressure, and temperature, then waited for the doctor. After a bit of a wait (typical for a clinic with reduced fees), she came in with a paper that had the word "positive" written among other printed words. As she spoke, I could barely hear her explaining that the standard pregnancy test they administered came back positive and that my abdominal pain was caused by my uterus expanding. I was in a daze. I could hear her like she was in a different room speaking to someone else while I was engaged in a conversation in my head. "Pregnant? What the fuck!?" was all I heard over and over. She asked what I wanted to do, and I muttered that I didn't know. After she examined me, she let me know that I was only about four weeks along, so I had time to decide if I would carry the child to term. In the meantime, they would make sure I was healthy. This clinic was also a social services hub of sorts so by the time I left, I was on Medicaid, WIC, food stamps, and had a case worker appointment to be assessed for a TANF check (Temporary Aid to Needy Families). I was still stunned. I had a bag filled with pamphlets about prenatal and infant care plus paperwork explaining my benefits and a prescription for prenatal vitamins. It was a mild southern February afternoon, so I walked home to the rented house I shared with my friends. My best friends were out together so no one was home. I sat on the front steps, spread the pamphlets and papers out around me on the porch, and I just sat there. After a while, I paged my friends multiple times with 911 so they would not delay (yes, that was the tail end of the pager era). It wasn't long before they pulled up in what we called "The Green Machine," my friend's big four-door green gas-guzzler sedan. "What's wrong!? What happened!?," they asked concerned. I just sat there, dazed and speechless. They looked around at the papers and put two and two together. I was pregnant! During the next few weeks, I had several sincere talks with God about what to do. I had already terminated a pregnancy by the same boyfriend four years earlier and was still plagued with guilt. I was in college and barely thriving. Due to my depression, I often isolated myself and missed classes resulting in WF grades (withdrawal fails). The same isolation pattern would resurface with jobs, so I wasn't financially stable. I still received bailouts from my parents and lived off student loans (which I so regret now). I was in Atlanta, 800 miles away from my family and hometown of Chicago, but I knew I would not move back there. It felt like I had barely survived living in Chicago without successfully committing suicide, so I had no desire to return to ground zero. I knew the baby's father was far from stable and not likely to be a good co-parent that I or the baby could depend on. Ultimately, I chose to keep the baby and in doing so, I consciously chose to be a single mother and raise her on my own. For me, that meant I had to finish school, whatever it took. I took the welfare, the maximum amount of student loans, and an overload of course credits each semester while pregnant. I attended class until I gave birth in November 1995 and was back in class two weeks later with a quiet baby girl chilling in her carrier. I graduated with my Bachelor of Arts in May 1996 when she was eight months old and got off welfare three months later when I accepted a job offer and moved into an apartment with no roommates. I was acutely aware that as I cashed my TANF check or used my food stamps or WIC vouchers, no one knew or cared that I was in college and that I didn't align to the stereotype of the Welfare Queen. When I went for prenatal checkups, I was simply another unwed pregnant Black woman on welfare and in some ways that was fine with me. The system so readily defines us by the Welfare Queen stereotype that it was easy to accept it, despite my intellectual understanding of welfare as a tool and safety net. Accepting welfare enabled me to get the help I needed while I worked to achieve my goal of finishing school. I didn't realize how much it had seeped into my consciousness. Politicians and the media defined the term Welfare Queen, so I was quite aware of society's definition. In fact, I bought into this stereotype and used it to judge myself and others as I assumed society viewed me: lazy, unintelligent, and promiscuous. When I used food stamps, I was aware of the looks I would get from people depending on whether I was in a nice grocery store with quality meats and produce (annoyed or judging) or a corner store in the hood (not a second look unless they wanted to sell, buy, or steal the food stamps). On the surface, I didn't seem to care and was glad to have the additional resources, I had no idea what people really thought about me and it wasn't my business anyway. However, deep down I wanted people, specifically my mother, to know this wasn't my life and that it wasn't permanent.

My mother was the only person who ever called me a Welfare Queen. I can't recall the exact conversation or when it happened. Perhaps it was soon after I told her I was pregnant and didn't know what I was going to do. Maybe it was after I gave birth and she worried that I wouldn't finish school. Or it could have been at any point that she was angry or worried about the life choices I was making and how difficult I was making my road ahead. Still, her motivation for saying it matters little and the circumstances or context matters even less. What I have come to understand is that it was hurtful and seared into my mind that this is how people would see me. My mother was afraid for me and her fear led her to those words in a misguided attempt to motivate me much like our ancestors when they used "Plantation Proverbs" to help guide us. That external motivation turned into internal pressure to prove that not only was I not a Welfare Queen, but that I also wasn't a typical single mother statistic.

As I mentioned, both the Welfare Queen and the Single Mother are a blend of Jezebel and Mammy, just in different proportions. Single mothers are often viewed as noble and self-sacrificing with no need for relationships other than her children. She is oddly desexualized, but her identity is predicated on being a mother as a result of sex before marriage, thus this stereotype is a bit more Mammy-dominant than Jezebel. Society pities her and yet pats her on the back for "doing it alone." These accolades can become an addiction and a self-fulfilling prophecy. After years of saying to myself, "I'm a strong woman, I can do this on my own," I started creating situations to prove I was strong, reinforcing that I was doing it alone, all in a subconscious effort to counteract perceptions about single mothers.

In 1996, after a year as a Welfare Queen, I started my journey with the new mask of Strong Single Mother. Fresh out of college, living alone, working, and raising an infant required more from me than I had ever given to anything or anyone including myself. I loved my little baby girl and wanted her to be safe and feel loved. I worked, I didn't date or party, and rarely socialized. I didn't have childcare other than the home daycare she attended while I was at work, so I had no options for a break other than her nap time. My social activities included my daughter and would end as we approached her 8pm bedtime. It continued like that for a year until I went to graduate school and my sister moved to Atlanta with her two children. We shared a duplex and helped each other raise our children. With her support, I was able to complete my MBA and accepted a corporate job in New Jersey that moved us all at their expense. I had solidly "upgraded" from Welfare Queen to Strong Single Mother. I had the love of my daughter but being a single mother and a Black woman in corporate America with newly graduated MBA peers reminded me that I was an anomaly, and it pissed me off. I was angry with my daughter's biological father for leaving me to be mother and father. I felt abandoned and upset when my daughter asked why her daddy wasn't around and didn't keep his promises to her. At the same time, I felt prepared for single motherhood. I had the power of my Ancestral Mothers who survived so that I may exist. I had living examples in my mother and sisters who worked diligently to care for and provide for their children. I had "Plantation Proverbs" embedded in my consciousness, so I already accepted that I had to work at least twice as hard as everyone else. I drew on that legacy of strength to push forward and create a life for my child, but I lacked the self-care skills to do so consciously as this was not modeled for me.

Despite the tenacity it takes to raise children solo, Strong Single Mothers experience the pain of multiple stereotypical judgements. It seemed that I was less attractive than the European standard of beauty while self-sacrificing as Mammy and disrespected as a Jezebel. All this, regardless if I was a business professional with a master's degree or a fulltime student collecting welfare. It seemed that society did not offer any good choices for a Black woman's identity and it hurt. I grew a shell of anger around the hurt that allowed me to ignore my emotions and push forward, always two steps from being pissed off.

Sapphire (aka The Angry Black Woman) and the Curse of Romance Novels

When I was growing up, my favorite thing to do (besides watch TV) was to read. I would polish off a book every day or two and was always headed to the mall to buy more. I hid under the covers at night reading with a flashlight. I read in the car or I would find a spot to settle in at my parents store to read between helping with customers. Reading was my passion. I found my escape in the pages of my books. I played mind movies with the scenes, plots and characters and they often seemed more real to me than my actual life. It seemed to me that books offered a view of real possibilities, where people, places, things, situations, and relationships set examples for how they should be in real life. My books, along with TV, were how I understood the world and where I could fit in it. On one hand, I had fallen in love with Maya Angelou's books and poems, which inspired me to believe I could accomplish anything and overcome anything. They also confirmed a sadness that there would always be some adversity to overcome as a Black woman, and there would be people who didn't respect my mind or admire my looks. I also learned from Sista Angelou that any elegance and poise I displayed would be innate and self-generated, not dependent upon someone else's determination. Unfortunately, this lesson would get drowned out by the TV shows and music videos I watched along with books that were far from the literary ranks of Maya Angelou. Whether it was the *Sweet Valley High* series written for teens, the Harlequin novels for adults, or even Jackie Collins' books for the drama seekers, I was enthralled by romance novels. These books painted a picture of what I believed true love looked like and how romance should show up in my life. True love would always think you are beautiful and never really get angry with you. True love would take you on amazing dates, fancy dinners, exciting concerts, out on the town dancing, or romantic picnics. True love would always lust for you, be willing to do anything to make you happy, and always find you exciting and sexy. True love would take care of you when you are sick and know what you needed and wanted before you even asked.

Over time, these fake unrealistic depictions of romantic love became the standard by which I assessed if I was being truly loved by my mate. These standards were one of the ways I shielded myself from vulnerability and the only way I thought romantic love could be real. When love didn't show up the way I expected it to and according to these standards, I was deeply disappointed and sad. More than that, I was angry. For years, I was the legendary angry Black woman. Not constantly in a state of anger, but always on guard for the ill treatment or disregard that would prove I wasn't being valued or loved correctly. I was ever vigilant, sensitive to any deviation from the true love standard set by the characters in my favorite books. I was always prepared and ready to correct my man, so he would love me in a way that would allow me to feel like the amazingly lovable and happy women in my romance novels. This angry persona was part stereotype and part reality. I used anger to cope with the fear and shame of not knowing how to define myself as a Black woman, that part is real. But not all Black women are angry and when we are, it is often justified and not to be dismissed as a stereotypical reaction. We have seen this stereotype for decades; some call her "Sapphire" after a character on the *Amos and Andy Show*. Others generically call her "Matriarch." On the TV shows of my youth, I saw her as Aunt Esther on *Sanford and Son*. This character exchanged harsh words with her brother-in-law Fred, and to a lesser degree, her own husband Woodrow. The main attributes of this stereotype include a lack of femininity while using masculine energy to control her children and emasculate her man. Sapphire isn't nice or supportive the way Mammy was towards her white family; she is harsh and demeaning, mostly to her own family. In these examples depicted on television, this Black woman was angry because her male mate did not measure up to her standards, so she overused her own masculine energy to compensate. Without her nagging or prodding, her man would never live up to his full potential and her needs would never be met. However, to say all Black women are perpetually angry for no reason is to belittle the real emotions at the root of our anger. Many Black women are angry and some for good reason. It's hard out here for sistas and it has been for centuries. But I can honestly say, without extrapolating to all Black women, that I have been an angry Black woman as a defense mechanism to hide my fear, my shame, my sadness.

If my mate didn't express undying storybook love for me, show up in my life with grand romantic gestures, or wasn't attentive and affectionate, then I didn't feel loved. I couldn't recognize love if it didn't show up like my romance novel characters, yet I craved it because I didn't know how to fill up on Divine love or self-love. Today, I strive to keep my Divine love tank full by spending time in my favorite spots in nature, like lakes, rivers, or mountains. I meditate and breathe deeply and admire the beauty God has created. I am reminded that I am one of God's creations as well, so how beautiful must I be! I also stay full on self-love through small daily rituals, doing things that bring me joy and saying no to things that don't. Before I understood that I am the source of love in my life, I was like an addict who needed a continuous fix from outside sources. At a subconscious level, I felt deeply fearful that love didn't show up like in my books because I was wasn't worthy of love. I feared I was just an asexual undesirable Mammy and former Welfare Queen who didn't look like Bunny DeBarge and wasn't sexy enough to be a video vixen. Searching for the experience of love with a premixed recipe in mind resulted in sadness and fear that I would never have the great love I knew to exist in the world as evidenced by my books. I didn't have the tools to simply feel my fear and allow it to pass like emotions inevitably do. Instead, I attempted to control as many variables in my life as possible to avoid painful feelings. Without conscious effort, I would be mean and critical or dismissive and emasculating to keep the fear of not being loved at bay. I thought letting my mates know what they were doing wrong was letting my needs be known and if I didn't, my needs would never be met. Or even worse, if my man didn't love me the "right" way, it would be proof that I was unlovable.

You would think I matured out of this as I aged, but I didn't. Even though as an adult, it was clear that love and relationships don't happen like in romance novels, it would still take me decades to stop expecting it to and to stop being angry about it. Sapphire or "Angry Black Woman" was my last line of defense against the pain of accepting my lot as "Fat, Black, Unlovable." Once I stopped being angry, there was nothing masking my fear and pain. I had to face them, and they nearly broke my heart.

Who am I?

In many ways I am all these stereotypes and yet something completely different. My soul has lived many lives on this earth within various vessels. I'm sure I have been a matriarch who nurtured her children and all those in her presence. After all, Yemoja is the Spirit of the Ocean and Mother of All. Because she loves her children, she is resourceful to ensure her children have life, whether that means being a stay-at-home mama, a single working mama, or a mama on welfare. I can assert that I have also been a sensual woman who was able to entice men with the prospect of tasting my honey. I enjoyed every minute of it just as Oṣùn, the Goddess of Love, enjoyed bringing Ogun back to civilization. Furthermore, I have no doubt that I have been a fierce, angry warrior, fighting for humanity against injustice. I have brought the winds of change much like Oya, the Goddess of Transformation. I can even imagine that one of my incarnations on earth was as a white woman, perhaps Master Granberry's mother and my 4th great-grandmother. The bottom line is that these are all aspects of me, of all Black women, but not the exaggerated one-dimensional characters created by colonizers and enslavers. The complexity of being a Black woman cannot be distilled down then poured into a mold and sold as trinkets. To truly understand Black women is to realize that we cannot be defined because we are the mothers of humanity, the essence of attraction and sensuality, and the spirit of change and transitions. Thus, only we can define ourselves, moment to moment, for only we know all these aspects of ourselves, which are in constant flux.

So, who am I now?

I strive to be a woman who is no longer defined by others. I refuse to be placed in a box or reduced to a caricature. I am many things. A mother, a sister, a daughter, a wife/partner, a woman, a warrior, a goddess, a princess, a dancer, a creator, a traveler, and a Spirit. I am all these and more with infinite qualities of funny, kind, adventurous, sensuous, gifted, smart, courageous, helpful, nurturing, supportive, honest, trustworthy, loving, lovable, likable, attractive, generous, thoughtful, joyful, light-hearted, cheerful, friendly, open-minded, expressive, creative, vivacious, and Spiritual. I am all these and more, I simply must do *The Work* to allow them to shine.

CHAPTER 4

Transformation Ain't Easy: You Gotta Do *The Work*

Each person is born with the responsibility to resolve their suffering and develop wisdom, even if the healing extends into their next lifetime, after death. Unless pain is dealt with directly, it seeps into our bodies creating dis-ease that affects our health and saturates our minds, creating shadows and false realities that undermine our fulfillment. To manage the pain of believing I was "Fat, Black, and Unlovable," living my life according to "Plantation Proverbs," and defining myself according to stereotypes, I put on a mask or suit of emotional armor to filter the pain and seemingly protect myself from being vulnerable. But, this mask, this full suit of armor once utilized as a short-term strategy to bear pain, was not sustainable and became a source of even more pain. The armor and the metastasized ache combined into a toxic potion that coursed through my veins, threatening to send me to an early grave. Emotional armor and pain can become legacies left behind for our children to contend with in their own lives, from mother to daughter, from father to son.

I inherited many methods of emotional self-protection from my mother. My armor and pain were always present, but her transition to the Ancestor Realm was like a supernova, ending her physical existence while illuminating possibilities for my life. It was the summer of 2006 and I was living in Atlanta with my kids and husband. I was at work when I got a call from my sister that my mother had been rushed to the hospital in Chicago. Her health crisis started when my parents were leaving the house to meet my oldest sister for her pre-birthday dinner before they left town to come visit me. My mother was in the car and my father was closing the garage door when suddenly it seemed as if she was having seizures of some sort. My father called 911 as soon as he looked at her and saw her struggling to breathe and a look of terror in her eyes. The ambulance got to my parents' house in record time and the doctors said she was having heart seizures because her heart was not holding the necessary electrical pulses to produce normal heart beats. She died 24 hours later, and the autopsy report concluded that her heart was quite enlarged—three times its normal size—likely due to prolonged and untreated high blood pressure. July 15, 2006 at 3:20pm my mother Quessie Maxine (Ingram) Williams made her transition on the same day her first born child (my sister) turned 50 years old. That night, we were all in the backyard escaping the summer heat and the lack of air-conditioning in the house. We told stories about her and remembered her while sitting among the flowers she planted and cared for so much. Then as I looked up at the sky from our backyard, I saw a large white bird fly overhead and I was immediately comforted. I knew that was a message from her spirit to let us know she would always be with us, each of us individually and all of us collectively. My ancestral support is strong, always guiding and protecting. I only have to listen.

And boy did I need to listen, not only to the whispers of my mama and other ancestors, but also to the messages from my own body. For years it has been screaming at me to make changes towards good health. Our bodies feel and absorb emotional pain and, when we don't process it fully, store it to be dealt with later. All the stress, all the beliefs that I wasn't enough, that I had to work harder, that I was unattractive, undesirable, and unworthy lay there in my tissue. The guilt, grief, and mourning I was born into fermented in my cells. All the trauma, cruelty, and oppression experienced by my ancestors and passed through epigenetics were imprinted in my DNA. All the negative thoughts about myself and the projected thoughts I assumed were coming from others circulated through my veins. The core foundational belief of myself as "Fat, Black, and Unlovable" was woven into the fascia holding my muscles together. All this emotional junk was held in my body, impairing optimal function, causing high blood pressure, inflammation, over stimulated nervous system, digestion issues, weakened immune system, hormonal imbalances, and recurring migraines. I didn't take these annoying health issues seriously, either ignoring them or pacifying them with ibuprofen, food, or clove cigarettes along with melatonin, wine, or weed at night to sleep and Red Bull in the morning to awaken. I lived my life so in my head, that I couldn't hear my body crying out to be cared for. In fact, I didn't even know what self-care really meant. Even after my mother's transition and knowing her death was related to heart disease, I only paid attention to my heart for a few years, getting checkups with a cardiologist and regular stress tests and EKGs. But eventually, I stopped taking my blood pressure meds; I didn't like how they made me feel and I didn't like the idea of taking prescription drugs regularly. When all my sisters' health declined in various ways—paralysis from strokes and heart attacks, brain aneurysm and COPD, and a brain tumor—I took steps to de-stress my life. I made healthier food choices, became more active, and lost 20 pounds over two years. Once I focused more on my spiritual life and started learning about traditional African spiritual systems, I dropped another 40 pounds over six months. I felt more energized and healthier that I ever had, but I wasn't checking my blood pressure regularly. All was good, until one morning in the fall of 2017. I walked out of my bathroom and suddenly had a sharp pain in my chest. It felt like lightening hit me in the heart, moved down through my body, out my rectum, and back around to my chest again repeatedly. I did all the mental checks for heart attack or stroke; I knew it wasn't those. My instinct was to drop to the floor, not because I couldn't stand, but because I felt better supported, more grounded. My husband was in the backyard and I managed to knock on a wall to get his attention. I could describe to him the pain I was feeling, but I could not identify what was happening to me. My husband called 911 and the ambulance got me to the nearest hospital. After being examined and tested at the hospital, they agreed that I was not having a heart attack or stroke, so they thought it might have been gas as well. I was given drugs for indigestion and powerful pain medications. They only administered half the typical dose of the pain meds at the request of my husband who had done a quick search on the side effects. After some time passed, they were preparing my discharge paperwork when the E.R. doctor checked in on me to see how I was feeling. My pain level hadn't changed which was puzzling to him; they were powerful drugs that should have reduced my symptoms even with the lower dosage. He told us he wanted to do one more test before I went home, to rule out a possible, but unlikely diagnosis. I remember sitting on the examination table while he pulled out a Sharpie and drew a picture of a heart and aorta directly on the sheet next me. It was a rare occurrence called an aortic dissection. Imagine your heart as a central pump whose job it is to process and distribute blood throughout your body. The aorta is the main pipe that exits up out the top of the heart then loops down so it is the shape of a candy cane. That main pipe is made of three layers of tissue (like 2-ply toilet tissue but 3-ply). The doctor thought that it was possible the inner layer of my 3-ply aorta tore, creating an opening that allowed blood to enter between the inner and middle layers and creating a double barrel of blood flow (the technical term is false lumen) rather than the normal single channel (true lumen). The test ordered was a CT scan and it required additional release forms since the test itself had its own risks. I took the test and we waited for the results, but emotionally we were just waiting to go home. Although the doctor described it as a possible diagnosis, he doubted that it would be confirmed because of how I was presenting. I was awake, coherent, and able to walk and answer questions. I had zoned out a few times at home, bad enough to let my husband know he needed to call 911 but, had never lost consciousness. My husband says he and the doctor were chatting when the doctor's phone rang with results of my test. Within seconds of answering that call, the doctor's face went from relaxed and friendly to pale, focused, and concerned. I was diagnosed with a Type A aortic dissection, the type that required immediate emergency open-heart surgery to repair it and save my life. The location of the tear (in the arch of my aorta) and the extent of the dissection (up into my carotid arteries in my neck all the way down into the iliac arteries in my abdomen) made it a particularly difficult surgery with a 50/50 prognosis. I survived the 10-hour surgery where a portion of my aorta was replaced with a tube of synthetic material called Dacron. I spent the next 50 days in intensive care, recovering, surviving, and dying, over and over.

At times when I was in recovery mode, I would lay in the hospital bed wishing I had understood my anatomy and truly comprehended the serious consequences of heart disease. For a while, I was angry that my body betrayed me after I made healthy lifestyle changes. But I realized that diet, exercise, and even weight loss, was like pouring a delicious nutrient-dense vegetable soup into a moldy bowl caked with spoiled food from years of usage without cleaning. A kind nurse suggested that my weight loss and improved fitness may not have stopped this from happening but may have been a factor in my survival. Healthy lifestyle and physical changes help us to combat chronic disease and aging while healing past trauma and cleansing our minds of the lies we have accepted as truth, allow the healthy life choices to happen organically. A healthy mind together with a lighter spirit can help you make decisions that heal your physical body and return it to its blueprint of optimal health. I changed how I ate, lost a good amount of weight, was exercising and more fit than I had been in decades. I was tapping into my higher consciousness and ancestral support as well as transforming my thought patterns. However, "Plantation Proverbs" and Black women stereotypes were difficult to excavate. The mental and physical effects of my deepest belief, "Fat, Black, and Unlovable" was still lurking. Eradicating this toxic belief was essential to my survival.

I have spent my life trying different modalities to heal my mind in hopes of creating a joyous life free of anxiety and depression. I tried different types of mental health systems like cognitive therapy, hypnotherapy, even anti-depression and anti-anxiety drugs. I studied ancient energy healing systems such as Reiki, practiced yoga, and meditated. I trained in Mindfulness Based Stress Reduction (MBSR). I have incorporated crystals, essential oils, and herbal medicine into my daily lifestyle. I read and listened to countless self-help and spiritual books, watched hours of videos, and took months' worth of workshops and trainings. I am a certified Change Management Practitioner so I'm an expert at helping organizations with the people-side of change. And I am currently in a certification program to be an intimacy coach and training to be a Pilates instructor. Until now, lasting transformation escaped me because I bounced around learning these things through trial and error with no clear idea of how to apply what I learned. I had setbacks that discouraged me and reconfirmed the deep-seated beliefs that were causing me pain in the first place. To help ensure I stay consistent with my healing journey, I distilled my experiences into to a set of daily, weekly and monthly practices. I refer to these suggested practices as *The Work* and they fall into five categories:

Five Components of *The Work*

Micro Moments Simple breathing techniques and meditations to do throughout the day for five minutes at a time, relevant for both the novice and experienced. These *Micro Moments* are calming and grounding while creating mental space and energy for transformation. Implementing techniques in small increments helps us to be consistent with our work which is the key to enduring improvements in our lives. If you don't try any other technique of *The Work*, *Micro Moments* alone can help improve your mental, emotional, and physical life – five minutes at a time. Without these practices, I find that my mental and emotional wellbeing are more susceptible to external influences. When I first started implementing these mini practices, I often let the stresses of modern adult life (or a self-sabotaging ego) distract me from taking these moments. It helped tremendously to set mobile phone alarms to remind me to do the practices throughout the day until it became second nature. I also use different timer apps and sounds on my mobile phone to ensure I spend at least five minutes doing the practice without checking the clock. I recommend picking soft pleasing timer sounds; getting jarred out of breathwork or meditation is counterproductive. I like flute, chime, or gong sounds.

Journal Your Journey For at least 20 minutes, two to three times a week, do focused writing to explore your inner thoughts and extract the beliefs that drive your perceptions. Specific topics or questions to explore are provided for each set of practices that follow. There are no rules except to express your true thoughts and feelings. You can write sentences as they surface, either as paragraphs or simple bullet points or use mind mapping instead of sentences. A mind map is a way to visually organize your thoughts. There are many books and websites that explain mind mapping in depth, so I will share only the main elements here. Start with an initial word or idea that comes up for you in response to the prompts provided. Write that central idea in the center of your journal page then branch out with secondary ideas with images or words that relate directly to the central concept. Each of the secondary ideas has related concepts that would be explored and mapped as well. Personally, I use all three methods of journaling: sentences, bullets, and mind maps. The point is to use this framework to let your thoughts and feelings flow on to paper without being encumbered by a rigid format.

Renew Your Wisdom Every month, take intentional actions like nature walks or craft projects that create connection with the inner most aspects of your body, mind, and spirit. We find replenishment by deepening our awareness of both physical and ethereal aspects of self. The goal of the practices suggested in *The Work* is to increase access to the timeless wisdom of nature, our ancestors, and our higher selves.

Nourish Your Mind Occasionally take time to be curious about yourself and establish a broader perspective of your life. Leverage the internet and modern technology to do simple research to learn about your ancient past and your possible future. As we clear away old programming, we must replace it with knowledge that has been obscured from our awareness for generations.

Celebrate Your Life Incorporate joy and play in your life as often as you can. Transformation and healing are best achieved through cycles of work, rest, and play. To heal, we must do the work to know ourselves, reflect and prepare, as well as release and revitalize. That effort must be honored by celebrating who we are in this moment, igniting our spirits and fueling us to be our best selves.

I use these five types of practices in different ways depending on the objective: awareness or forgiveness. The first step to lasting transformation is to be aware of the aspects of yourself that require change. Thus, we begin *The Work* with *Becoming Aware in Oṣùn 's Mirror* as detailed below in order to truly know thyself. After committing at *least* three months of *consistent* work on self-awareness, one is then ready to broaden that awareness to include family and intergenerational truths. *The Work: Walk A Mile Then Pivot* empowers us to own our stories and forgive our past while practicing perspective-taking. Each of these "works" has its own set of practices in the categories of *Micro Moments, Journal Your Journey, Renew, Nourish, and Celebrate.* The work you do in *Becoming Aware in Oṣùn 's Mirror* prepares you to go deeper and broader in *Walk a Mile Then Pivot.*

Collectively, *The Work* is not a set of dogmatic instructions or the outcome of scientific research. *The Work* is based on my experience with different techniques and is simply a set of guidelines and suggestions to start your journey. Make them your own. Play with them. Try some of them or all of them. Get together with a trusted friend, your sister circle, or your mate and share what you are learning or what works and doesn't work. Share your experience on the *Beautiful.Powerful.Love* Facebook page (https://www.facebook.com/beautifulpowerfullove/) to inspire others with your story. Transformation is both solitary and communal. Each person must do their own soul work, but we can learn from and support each other through that process.

Access Free Bonus Content To Help You On Your Journey

Scan QRCode or visit BeautifulPowerfulLove.com/book
Password: *goopwork256*

The Work: Becoming Aware in Oṣùn 's Mirror

Transformation demands sacrifice and we must be willing to give up something to realize our desires. For a new way to begin, an old way must be abandoned. Sometimes the sacrifice is how you spend your time or money, but it's always what you think and how you behave. Don't let, "That's just the way I am," hold you back from the life you desire. Real talk? That's a cop out and our egos or shadow selves can conspire to keep us complacent if we allow it to. It's true that we are born with certain traits and characteristics, but if the "way you are" blocks you from your good, then it's time to do a critical analysis of yourself. I often struggled to understand the true essence of my character versus the protection mechanisms of my constructed ego. Through the practices below, I strengthen my self-awareness to discern my true internal nature versus programming from the external world. Developing self-awareness is about knowing and accepting all aspects yourself. It is the critical first step to transformation as it helps us identify the lies we have accepted as fact. These are lies we not only told ourselves, but lies that friends, family, and society has told us as well. Ultimately, the goal of becoming aware is to enable us to distinguish truth from illusion. When I became aware of myself, I saw the false me that identified as "Fat, Black, an Unlovable" *and* I saw the true me that was *Beautiful. Powerful. Love.* Even though it was an illusion, seeing the false me was still a breakthrough of truth because it cut through all the mental distractions and articulated what I truly thought of myself, but was never able to admit. Through the practices and resources below, I was able to connect the "Plantation Proverbs," colonizer definitions, and family wounds to my core belief, creating a roadmap for my healing journey. I invite you to do the same for yourself, in your own way.

Micro Moments <u>Awareness breath</u>: You can do this at any time (except while driving). You can sit, lie down, or stand. Your hands can be palms up on your lap if you are sitting or down alongside your body if you are standing or on your chest and abdomen if you are laying down. I like to settle into my body first. Notice the feeling of the chair underneath you, where it touches your legs or notice the floor beneath your feet where you are standing. Relax your shoulders letting them fall, down and away from your ears. Then turn your attention to your breath. Don't change it, don't judge it, just notice it. Notice the feeling of air entering your nostrils. Follow where it goes. Does it go to the back of your throat? Don't try to adjust it. Just notice the breath. Notice what else is involved with the breath. Does your stomach move? Your ribs? Your chest? Notice all the parts of your body that move, expand, or contract with every inhale or exhale. Do this for at least 5 minutes, as many times a day as you need or want. Remember the point is just to become aware of your breath, which is simply bringing your attention to the essence of yourself. It takes practice; your mind might wander, but notice that too, then release it without beating yourself up and return your attention to your breath. If you feel especially anxious, after 5 minutes of just awareness of your breath with no alteration to it, start to consciously make your exhales longer than your inhales. Play with it, exhale for four counts then inhale for two counts or exhale for six counts then inhale for three counts. See what feels good and do that for 5 minutes. The longer exhales will help remove stagnant air and help signal the body to relax and let go.

Grounding: You can do this visualization mediation following awareness breath work or as a separate practice. This technique works best sitting or standing so that your feet are flat on the floor. I prefer to do this with shoes and socks off, but it can be effective even with shoes. It can be done in as little as five minutes, but if you are new to mediation or visualization, it may take a few weeks of practice to move through the entire technique as described below in five minutes. In each session, just set your timer for five minutes and you will still receive benefit even if the timer ends before you do the complete exercise. Close your eyes and take a few moments to connect with your breath, then focus on the sensations on the bottom of your feet. Don't force any foot movement, but as you bring attention to your feet, you may be inspired to stretch or flex your toes or arches. This may feel like a tingling or itch or perhaps no feeling at all. Rather than reacting to any tingling you may feel, imagine the sensation of tentacles of light growing from the soles of your feet. Each foot may have one tentacle or several. In either case, imagine the tentacles, not as physical appendages, but as rays of light extending out of your feet. These rays are not limited by your shoes or socks, so they easily exit your foot coverings. Use your imagination and physical senses to envision your rays of light extending into the floor or ground, surpassing the foundation of whatever structure you may be in (building, bus, car, etc.). Stay connected with the physical sensation on the soles of your feet as you imagine your rays of light easily moving through rock and dirt without harming anything along the way. Keep breathing and maintain awareness of your own body, particularly the soles of your feet and the sensations that may be developing. Continue penetrating your light tentacles deeper into the earth, passing through all the layers of crust, molten lava, and precious metals until you reach the huge hollow space surrounding the bright glowing core at the center of the earth. In your mind's eye, see the core's shining brilliance, full of light and beauty, and imagine its radiating warmth like the earth's internal sun. Imagine that as the light rays extending from the soles of your feet get closer to earth's brilliant core, it becomes more and more difficult to distinguish between the light particles of earth's core and those of your foot rays. See the light particles of your rays moving towards the earth's core, fueling it and helping it glow brighter and warmer (but not burning). Feel the warmth emanating from earth's core and imagine that sensation of warmth reaching the soles of your feet, energizing you from the tips of your toes to the top of your head. Imagine this relationship of extending yourself into the earth, fueling it with your brilliant light rays and receiving the warmth and glow from the earth throughout your body and mind. Cultivate the feeling of giving unconditionally and joyfully, yet receiving immediately and exponentially. Sit in that feeling for a few moments, imagining your deep connection to the earth through your light rays and the energy exchange taking place. Take three deep breaths, imagining the glow of earth's core expanding and contracting along with your lungs as you inhale and exhale slowly. Softly say "thank you" or think thoughts of gratitude and go about your day.

Journal Your Journey When you have at least 20 minutes to dedicate to your self-healing, do the awareness breath while looking in the mirror. It can be your bathroom mirror or a hand mirror but ensure you can clearly see your eyes and comfortably stay there for ten minutes. I wear glasses, but I take them off so that my view is unobstructed, and I adjust the lighting and my distance from the mirror in order to see more than a blur. For the first five minutes, focus on awareness of your breath as instructed in *Micro Moments*. Next, focus your attention only on your eyes. Look deeply into your own eyes, without judgement or evaluation. Notice the whites of your eyes, your pupils, and your iris. Become aware of the size, shape, and color of each part of your eye without assessing, just observing. Your eyes may drift away from their refection in the mirror to look at other parts of your face like your forehead or cheeks or even your eyelashes or dark circles under your eyes. When this happens, gently bring your eyes back to focus on themselves in the mirror, not the facial features surrounding them. You may notice changes in the eyes, perhaps they start to water, the whites turn reddish or the pupils dilate. Just notice the changes with a feeling of neutrality. No change is good or bad, it just is, and will soon evolve to yet another change. Do this for at least five minutes, but gaze into your eyes for as long as you would like.

If you find it difficult to spend time with yourself in this way, I suggest doing this mirror work a few times as its own practice to become comfortable with your reflection. The next step of your mirror session is to write in your journal, using any of the journaling methods described earlier in this chapter. At first, you can write whatever comes to mind following your mirror session. It doesn't have to make sense and you don't have to share it with anyone, but yourself. When you are comfortable with this process, next time do the same mirror work while holding a specific question in your mind and patiently waiting for the answer as you mirror gaze. The answer may not come immediately or at all during your mirror session. I find that these sessions with specific questions flow better if I release the question after asking it rather than continue to hold the question in my mind. I liken it to asking your teacher a question and being quiet to receive the answer. Our hope with journaling in this way is to connect with the eternal part of ourselves that knows the answer to any and every question we may have. We connect with our breath and eye gaze to bypass the ego and analytical mind and access our internal guidance system. We ask our question, a single question, with openness and a desire to receive the answer, and with certainty that it will come. Then we journal immediately, using whatever technique that works for us, with no expectations of the content and no judgement of the thoughts it reveals. Ask only one question per session to allow your consciousness to focus and increase the clarity of the answer received. This exercise should be done 2 – 3 times per week and I would focus on the same question (or variations of it) in all sessions that week or longer. You can ask any question you like, but I recommend exploring the following questions as a starting point:

1. Who am I?
2. Who do I think I am?
3. Who do I want to be?
4. Who do people think I am?
5. What do I believe about myself?
6. Which beliefs support and sustain me?
7. Which beliefs diminish and drain me?

Asking and journaling the same questions periodically to check in with myself as well as reading previous journal entries has been helpful in my journey. This cadence of updating and reflecting helps me identify thoughts or beliefs that persist, morph, and show up in different ways in my mind.

Renew Your Wisdom Explore five aspects of nature that are accessible and appeal to you. Connect with the natural element to uniquely experience it. For example, do you like water? Do you live near a river or waterfall? Go spend time there alone or with others that will support quiet time and introspection. Put your feet in the water or go for a dip if it's safe, do some stretches on the river bank, or have a seat and watch the waves or ripples. While you are there, do a few extended *Micro Moments*, connecting with the earth and the water in that particular place. If possible, peer at your reflection in the water and experiment with your mirror work. Next month, go spend time in a different aspect of nature like mountains or forests or even a different type of natural water like the ocean or a lake. Take a drive in the mountains, stop at a lookout point, and do your *Micro Moments* there. Take a rest against a tree during a hike through the forest or a walk in the park and do your *Micro Moments*. Sit on the beach, breathing with the ocean waves and doing your *Micro Moments*. You can sunbath in your backyard or admire the beauty of your houseplants. The point is to experience unique aspects of nature and observe how you feel during and after. While you are connecting with this element of nature, do you feel calm and relaxed and more easily able to do your awareness breath and grounding? Do you notice yourself breathing a little deeper in this place? Do you feel expansive after spending time in this space? Does your mind feel more alert, sharper? Do you have more creative ideas or feel less stressed and more at peace? Do you not notice a change at all? After a few months of this exercise, you would have spent intentional time in various elements of nature, learning what you like and what feeds your soul.

I live in Washington state surrounded by mountains, rivers, lakes, waterfalls, woods, and within a reasonable driving distance to the ocean, volcanoes, and temperate rainforests. I am blessed to have a diversity of nature I can explore within five-minutes to five-hours from my neighborhood. I also lived in Chicago, Atlanta, and Newark, which are much more densely populated and less abundant with untouched nature. If you live in an urban area, your mission is to seek out various elements of nature wherever you can, such as city parks, state parks, botanical gardens or even your backyard. Do some internet research to see what is reasonable for you to travel to and make plans to visit. Whether you take a bus across town to a waterfront park or carpool to the nearest state park, excursions into nature can happen as a part of our normal lives even if we live in urban areas.

Nourish Your Mind In this technique, we take our exploration of nature out of the physical world of experience into the mental world of intellectual knowledge. Consider all the places in nature you have connected with from *Renew Your Wisdom*. With which aspect of nature do you seem to connect with most strongly (I call it my sweet spot)? Where would you build your dream home so that you maximize time in this special place? Maybe a cabin in the woods, a chalet in the mountains, or perhaps an ocean beach house? Once you determine where your connection to nature is the strongest, start learning as much as you can about it. Search the internet for websites, videos, and images of your sweet spot. Visit the library and ask the librarian for help finding books and articles on your special place. For example, I connect deeply with water in nature. This includes oceans and lakes, but I am fascinated by rivers and waterfalls. As I recognized my strongest connection to nature, I set out to learn as much as I could about rivers and waterfalls in general and specifically those in my area. I conducted internet searches to find all the rivers near me, their specific location and accessibility. I researched how the rivers formed, what waterways fed into them and where they eventually deposit their bounty. I researched the ecology of the river: is it home to specific species of fish or animals, is it under environmental attack via pollution or is it relatively clean and unharmed? I noted the current name of the rivers and looked for names given to them by the original indigenous people in the area. I also read facts and folklore about sacred rivers in other countries like the Oṣùn River in Nigeria, the Nile River in Kemet, or the Narmada River in India. Through *Renew Your Wisdom*, I became aware of my connection to rivers through physical experience. With *Nourish Your Mind*, I became more knowledgeable of the characteristics of the rivers near me and around the world. The more I learn about rivers, the more I learn about myself and possibilities for managing my daily life. I begin to understand that we are literally a part of the earth and that I share characteristics with rivers and waterfalls.

After a few months of *Renew Your Wisdom* followed by taking time to *Nourish Your Mind*, go back to *Journal Your Journey* to do the mirror work and journaling session with the same reflective questions as before. Has anything changed? Do you see yourself differently? Do you see the world differently? Recognize any change with a sense of neutrality and don't be discouraged if there are none. Our unconscious thoughts and beliefs were programmed over generations and require time to be transformed. Don't give-up! Keep working at it and you will realize results. In the meantime, celebrate!

Celebrate Your Life You have worked with Oṣùn 's Mirror and gained more awareness of yourself and your connection to nature. Celebrate yourself by finding ways to bring more of that connection into your daily life. Perhaps you treat yourself to fresh cut flowers when you shop for groceries. Or you print images of ocean waves or a beautiful waterfall to hang in your home or office. The idea is to create daily mini celebrations of your sweet spot (that place in nature that you are most deeply connected to) to invigorate you along your journey. Your celebration can include grand gestures of self-love like a trip to Nigeria to experience the energy of the Oṣùn River or a mountain adventure in the serene Himalayas. However, we can't wait for the finances and time to reward ourselves with travel to our natural sweet spot, we must refuel ourselves throughout the day, every day. *Celebrate Your Life* is a critical component of becoming aware. It is the rejuvenation that eases the discomfort of transformation while powering us to keep going forward.

Relevant Resources:

- *Power of Vulnerability: Teachings of Authenticity, Connection, and Courage* by Dr. Brené Brown
- *Madly in Love with ME: The Daring Adventure of Becoming Your Own Best Friend* by Christine Arylo
- *The Value in the Valley: A Black Woman's Guide Through Life's Dilemmas* by Iyanla Vanzant

- *Meditations Across the King's River: African-Inspired Wisdom for Life's Journey* by James Weeks
- *Beyond Sex: Tantra - a practical guide to extraordinary living* by Tanja Diamond
- *Mirror Work: 21 Days to Heal Your Life* by Louise Hay
- www.palousemindfulness.com/ Free Online Mindfulness-Based Stress Reduction (MBSR) Course

The Work: Walk a Mile and Pivot

Becoming Aware in Oṣùn's Mirror helped to get you focused and in tune with the beliefs that shape your experiences. Some of what you uncovered may be indications of your true divine nature or simply the result of stories you have accepted subconsciously. It can be difficult to distinguish between stories and the truth since many of our beliefs seem to have been a part of us since birth. We are conceived through our parents as pure and untainted souls. During gestation in the womb as well as after birth, we are exposed to the emotions, thoughts, and energy of the mother and the people in the household. Whether a fetus, baby, or young child, children are like sponges with no filter, absorbing everything around them with no way to separate out what's bullshit and what's truth. Our trust in what we see and hear from our families is unwavering; all lessons, good or bad, go straight in and the child accepts the lesson, thought, or belief as their own. I came to understand this during my early days of therapy and reacted emotionally with repressed anger. "Why didn't they think, say, or do something different? Why did they let me feel and think this way?" I thought. It took doing *The Work* below to realize my anger towards my parents was not only pointless, but also harmful. While it is important to acknowledge the emotion of anger, there is no point to *being* angry because it can't change the past, only ruin the present, and possibly taint the future. However, we often must move through anger to get to the healing salve of forgiveness and gratitude. I understood the importance of forgiveness and gratitude intellectually, but it was hard to do if my rational mind would not agree. I had to understand my parents from their perspective, rather my own as their child. I had to realize that my parents existed before my birth, with lives filled with joy, pain, dreams, and setbacks as individuals and as a couple. Through compassionate exploration of my family stories, I could acknowledge not only my anger, but also my pain and fear, and see them as wounds resulting from good intentions. More importantly, I could acknowledge and empathize with my parents' wounds. This combination of acknowledgement, compassion, and empathy will allow you to reframe your family stories with forgiveness and gratitude. The practices below invite you to take an emotional swan dive into the beliefs you learned from family or caregivers. *The Work: Walk a Mile and Pivot* builds upon the progress in self-awareness made in *The Work: Becoming Aware in Oṣùn's Mirror.* Continuing the self-awareness practices will sustain you on what may be a difficult journey.

Micro Moments Dynamic conscious breath: This breathwork should be done standing or sitting, not laying down. Start with a long exhale out of your mouth, drawing in your abdomen as much as you can and bending slightly to help push out as much air as possible. Just when you think you have expelled all the air in your lungs, pull in your abdominal muscles and pull up your diaphragm a bit more, pushing out stagnant air from deep in your lungs. Then inhale through your nose by releasing the muscular contraction around your core and rising from the bent position. Allow air to flow back into your lungs naturally, as your core relaxes creating space within your body for air. As you inhale, further relax your abdomen allowing it to expand outward. This may be a challenge for those accustomed to holding their stomachs in, but it is critical to learn to let go and allow this expansion with breath. With each open-mouth exhale, slowly force out every bit of air from your lungs, each time activating deeper core muscles to push air out. Many of us do not typically breathe this deeply so the rush of oxygen may make you feel light headed at first. If this happens, simply return to normal breath for a minute or two, until you feel clear then return to this practice for the remainder of the five minutes. As you grow accustomed to this way of breathing, imagine you are pulling a corset around your mid-section, contracting the front, sides, and back of your core when you exhale, and expanding your core in the front, sides, and back of your body like a balloon when you inhale. As you increase your awareness of your core muscles, think of them collectively as an internal cylinder. As you exhale, actively pull in the deep core muscles that wrap around to your back, while contracting and lifting your diaphragm (top of cylinder) and pelvic floor (bottom of cylinder). As you inhale, completely relax your core muscles to allow your lungs more room to expand. As with all *Micro Moments,* continue this pattern of exaggerated exhaling and inhaling for at least five minutes. Consciously activating our core muscles while breathing will help release stale air from deep in your lungs and calm your nervous system. I have found this breath technique to be both energizing and relaxing, depending on what my body needs at the time. It has been a particularly beneficial tool during times of high stress or extreme emotions, helping me move through the experience without developing new emotional triggers.

Body scan: This technique can be done sitting, standing, or laying down. It can be done anytime, but when you are just starting this practice, it's best to do at a time when you can close your eyes. Take a few moments of awareness breath then turn your attention to your left big toe

Feel the sensations in your big toe. You may feel a pulsing sensation or tingling. Move your attention to each toe, feeling whatever there is to feel. Not searching or forcing, but simply bringing awareness to what is there. If you have on socks, what does the fabric feel like on your foot? Is it soft or scratchy? If you are barefoot, feel the air on your skin. Notice the temperature; is your foot warm or cold? Feel the sensations of your foot, both the top and bottom as well as the arches. Focus your mind on your ankle, then your calf and shins. Maintain your breath as you become aware of each body part, moving up your leg until you reach your knee. Observe any sensations there, then move on to the front of your thigh, the back of your thigh, your outer thigh, and inner thigh. What sensations can you detect? Is there any tenderness, fatigue, or sensation of temperature? Continue surveying your thigh until you reach your pelvic bone then switch your attention over to your right big toe. Start the process again feeling any sensations of temperature, pulsating, or twitching. Slowly move your attention up from your toes to your foot then your right ankle. Observe your shin and calf muscles to your knee and all the inner workings of your right knee. Focus on your right thigh, front, back, inner, and outer, until you reach your pelvis again. Observe sensations of your pelvic region including your reproductive organs, pelvic bone, and pelvic floor muscles. Move on to your derriere. Any sensations to notice in your buttocks? What does the chair, floor, or bed feel like underneath you as you sit or lay down? Pay attention to every sensation, but keep your awareness moving up to your lower back. Do you feel any big sensations like pain or strain or is what you feel subtler? How do the sensations change as you focus on your mid back, upper back, and shoulder blades? Now bring your attention to the front of your body and core. There are so many body parts to pay attention to in your core whether it's the skin or muscles or various elements of your digestive system. Scan your core for any sensations. Move your awareness up through your chest— skin, breasts, nipples, or muscle and notice what you feel. Take some time to connect with your heart. Can you detect its pumping motion? Keep moving your attention until you reach your collarbone then switch your focus to the fingertips of your left hand. Are your fingertips cold or warm? Can you feel the blood flow in your fingers? Continue moving your attention through your hand to your wrist and forearm then observe anything you feel in your left elbow before moving on to your biceps and triceps. Once you reach your left shoulder, switch your attention to the fingers on your right hand. Repeat this process; scan your right fingers, hand, wrist, forearm, bicep, and triceps up to your right shoulder. Then move your attention across both shoulders and trapezius muscles simultaneously until you reach your neck. Observe any physical sensations of the front, sides, and back of your neck as well as your throat. Shift your awareness to your face, starting with your chin and jawline, moving up to the sides of your face while observing any sensation. Scan your ears, then cheeks and nose before moving on to your eyes. How do your eyes feel? Are they tired, or burning, or dry, or watery? What about your eyebrows and forehead, any sensations there? Now focus on the back and sides of your head, any tingling or perhaps itching? Whatever sensation you feel, just recognize it, observe it. Survey each part of your head and scalp until you reach the very top of your head. Rest there for a moment and just feel any sensations. The first few times you do this, it may take more than five minutes to complete the full body scan. Work with whatever amount of time you have. If you can only spend five minutes, move your awareness through your body quickly, without dwelling on any particular part. If you have more time, take it a bit slower and scan a bit deeper. You may get distracted as you do this body scan. When you notice that your mind has drifted, just bring it back to your body scan. Each time you do the scan, you strengthen your ability to maintain focus on your internal physical experiences. With regular use of this technique, I have gained greater awareness of the chemical and hormonal changes in my body in direct response to outside stimulus as well as increased my ability to choose how the stimulus affects me.

Journal Your Journey For this technique, we continue the practices started in *Becoming Aware in Oṣùn's Mirror*, starting with five minutes of awareness breath. Connecting with your breath is always a good place to start any endeavor. By now we have been working with our mirror reflection for a few months, so we can start eye gazing while holding this question in mind: What lessons have your parents, family elders, or caregivers taught you (either verbally, by example, by their actions, or by their absence)? Spend five to ten minutes eye gazing while holding this question in your mind. Then release the question and let whatever thoughts that come up, flow out of your mind and onto the pages of your journal. This may be a difficult topic. The writing exercise could bring up both your known and unknown triggers. Use the *Micro Moment* techniques to work through any big emotions that arise. Repeat this process with the same question for a few weeks. Relationships in our family of origin are often complexly layered and can be riddled with unconscious trauma and suppressed anger. Take as much time as you need to explore this question with honesty and empathy, seeking only to understand and release.

After a few weeks or months of examining the life lessons derived from family, choose one specific lesson that has been a major driver in your life. Almost every lesson is attached to multiple stories that formed and reinforced it. What is the story behind your biggest family lesson? Choose one story and journal the details with this slightly structured approach:

1. Clearly identify who the catalyst was in this story. Was it your mother, your father, a grandparent, or a caregiver? I found that my memory often coagulates past experiences making it difficult to see each experience as its own and each person involved as separate entities. Do your best.

2. What did this person say in this specific story? Your investigation is looking for the person's actual words in this story, not what they "always used to say" or someone else said, and they agreed. Can you remember the exact words they used? Were they talking to you or did you observe or overhear what was said? What was their tone and facial expression as they said it? Only write the facts of the person's verbal and nonverbal communication that you observed with your ears and eyes, with no judgement or filters applied.

3. What did this person do? In this same story, did this person do anything in addition to saying something? Describe the facts of their actions, without judgement or filters or attempting to explain why they did it.

4. What did you think? While this person was saying the words or doing the actions, what were you thinking? What about immediately after the "incident," what did you think then? Do your best to remember your thoughts with accuracy, being honest about your thoughts *at* the time versus your thoughts *about* the time.

5. How did you feel? When the events of this story were taking place, how did your body feel? Use the skill of body scanning to go back in time to remember what major sensations you felt back then. Did your body temperature rise? Did you feel a lump in your throat or did your stomach get queasy? Try to remember how your body physically reacted to the experience in real time. Furthermore, what emotions did you feel? Were you excited, amused, sad, confused, or anxious? Again, this exploration is based only on your immediate physical and emotional responses at the time.

6. Now spend a few minutes in awareness breath to bring yourself out of the past in your mind, and back to your current reality. Use any of the other *Micro Moment* practices that you feel called to do to help you work with any emotions that have come up. Then as clearly as you can, write how you are responding now mentally, physically, and emotionally. Describe how you feel in your body, what emotions you currently have, and what thoughts come up in this moment.

7. Working with this same story, imagine some of the details are different from how you remember them. Perhaps the catalyst is a different person, or they said or did something different. The change could be what you

would have liked to have happened or something far worse than reality. With each of these changes, what impact might it have had on your thoughts as well as your physical and emotional states? What would change for you in this story based on different person doing or saying different things? How would changes to this story of the past affect you now? Your goal is not to negate the reality of what happened, but to explore a broad range of possibilities.

Use the process outlined above to examine different stories related to the same life lesson or stories related to different lessons. After a few months of working with your family stories, think about the people you identified as catalysts. Having thoroughly examined both the external facts and your mental, physical, and emotional outcomes, now you shift your perspective to the catalyst characters in the stories. Whether it was your parent, a caregiver, or a relative, what stories, beliefs, or life lessons might lie beneath their words or actions? Use your imagination to think of what they may have learned from their parents or caregivers. How might their hurtful words or deeds be extensions of their own pain? The purpose of this exercise is not to make excuses for the words and actions of others or to perpetuate a victim mentality. This process helped me to forgive the catalysts of my stories, my parents and elders who did or said something that created a wound and installed an emotional trigger within my consciousness. Gradually, I was able to reframe my stories, broadening my view to include the possibility of others' perspectives. As I continued this process, the life lessons, beliefs, and triggers created by these stories changed or dissolved. What resulted was natural empathy and forgiveness for others and gratitude for my new life lessons and perspectives.

Renew Your Wisdom Create a space for introspection and connection with your ancestors. This will be a sacred space dedicated to this purpose and steeped in your intention to heal and grow. Taking this action may be difficult if your relationship with your parents or family has been traumatizing and you are not ready to forgive. I encourage you to work with your *Micro Moments* and *Journaling Your Journey* exercises to help open your heart to this process of healing. Sacred ancestor space reveres all our honorable deceased relatives in our bloodlines who came before us, not only those that raised us as children.

Resources like *Jambalaya* by Yeye Luisah Teish go into more detail about ancestral veneration, so I will just share the basics based on my experience. Basic components of any ancestral altar include:

- Smudging stick (such as Palo Santo or white sage). First, select a location in your home that can be dedicated to this purpose like a small table, top of a bookcase, or even on the floor where it would not be stepped on or disturbed. Burn the smudging stick and allow the smoke to energetically cleanse the space.

- White cloth which can be a pillow case, a table cloth, or a piece of material from the fabric store. Place the cloth on the surface you have selected.

- A small plant or flowers placed on the white cloth as a representation of the earth.

- A white candle, any size whether it is as small as a tealight or a large pillar candle. Be careful not to leave the candle unattended while lit. You can also place the candle in a bowl of water to mitigate accidental fires.

- Pictures, names of deceased loved ones, family mementos, or artifacts.

I was taught to set up my altar with the left side representing the maternal side of my family and the right side representing the paternal side. From these basic instructions, use your creativity and instincts to personalize your ancestral space, adding whatever elements you feel called to add.

After setting up this space, use it regularly. Sit there and do morning prayers or one of your *Micro Moments* practices. I go to my ancestral alter daily to show gratitude and call the names of my relatives or commune with my mother in the Ancestral Realm. It has become my go-to space when I need to meditate on major decisions. The key is to connect with this ancestral space regularly to offer gratitude and ask for guidance when needed.

Nourish Your Mind The American educational system teaches a myopic Eurocentric view of history. Deepen your knowledge of your ancestral history. Research Black history in America, learning about the many enslaved African men and women who fought back against oppression and the many who excelled despite insurmountable circumstances. Learn about the Reconstruction Era, Jim Crow, and the Civil Rights Movement. Get the facts about the slave trade timeline and points of origin and destination. Understand which African countries or tribes were enslaved and the countries that profited from this forced global movement of people. Finally, if or when you can, invest in researching your DNA to gain insight into your own lost history. Use your DNA results as a starting point to research the African countries or tribes from which you descended.

Celebrate Your Life Host a dinner party! Invite friends or family over or make it a solo feast. Prepare a family dish, your favorite meal, or experiment with recipes from throughout the Diaspora such as Caribbean, Africa, Brazil, or even African-American soul food. Be sure to add a healthy twist, maybe reduce or eliminate salt, compensating with other herbs and spices or replace the sugar in recipes with stevia or monk fruit sweetener. Include raw or steamed vegetables with the meal. If cooking is not your thing, invite others to join in a Diaspora-themed potluck and commit to making at least one dish. Once all the food is prepared, but before the feasting begins, place a spoonful of each dish on a small plate and place it in your ancestral space.

Don't wait to have your dinner party during a major U.S. holiday or a birthday, though you can do it then too. Have your dinner party when you feel called to do so, making an ordinary day a special day for you. Culinary traditions are usually the last to be stripped away during forced assimilation. For many of our enslaved ancestors, the foods they created in the African Diaspora were not only for nutrition, but also a source of comfort as well as a necessary and critical reminder of home. These African culinary traditions were kept alive by our enslaved ancestors through adjustments to new ingredients and limited resources. Come together in community to celebrate yourself and our African ancestors who survived the Middle Passage to preserve our traditions.

Relevant Resources:

- *Jambalaya: The Natural Woman's Book of Personal Charms and Practical Rituals* by Luisah Teish
- *The Cooking Gene: A Journey Through African American Culinary History in the Old South* by Michael W. Twitty
- *The Isis Papers: The Keys to the Colors* by Dr. Frances Cress Welsing
- *Intuitive Self-Healing: Achieve Balance and Wellness Through the Body's Energy Centers* by Marie Manuchehri
- *The Celestine Prophecy: An Adventure* by James Redfield
- www.slavevoyages.org/ The Trans-Atlantic Slave Trade Database with information on almost 36,000 slaving voyages
- www.africanancestry.com/ DNA testing to determine your African country and ethnic group of origin
- www.africanbites.com/ Easy African and Caribbean recipes
- www.kitchenistadiaries.com/ Online recipes and/or cookbooks to order

CONCLUSION

Beautiful. Powerful. Love.

Transforming many lifetimes of thoughts that culminated in core beliefs spanning generations is no easy feat. I have taken huge strides, but soul work doesn't get to a place of total completion. Triggers are real, and we live in a world built on systemic oppression where everyone's self-identify is attacked daily no matter your race or gender. And from my perspective, this is especially and historically true for Black women since we can't access white privilege or gender bias as other groups can. However, even in the face of tyranny, we have a choice. We can choose to rewrite our "Plantation Proverbs," to glean a different perspective from the wisdom passed down. We can choose to reject the characterizations brutally administered upon us by colonizers and define ourselves in our own terms via our own measures. And we can acknowledge our wounds and heal them through forgiveness and release, for our own benefit and that of our bloodlines. These simple, yet profoundly impactful, and often difficult actions require commitment to yourself. Commitment to letting go, exploring, and rebuilding your inner world. It takes courage to retrain your brain to think differently and release pain. It takes time to stop a thought pattern and replace it with another or better yet, not replace it at all, but simply be done with mental stories. During that time of becoming, you don't know who you are or what you are. You are in the midst of transformation and it's like being in the *Void*. And it is the scariest shit ever.

This process of transforming beliefs is like a caterpillar transforming into a butterfly. Most people know that a caterpillar metamorphoses into a chrysalis before transforming into an adult butterfly. However, many people don't realize that inside that chrysalis, the caterpillar breaks down into a primordial goop. It ceases to be a caterpillar, but it is not yet a butterfly. A soupy goopy substance doesn't have to figure out what it will become and doesn't try to hang on to what it once was. It's just goop. Then, when the time is right, all the elements that were previously an egg, then a caterpillar, and now "goop" will reorganize itself according to the blueprint embedded in its genetic make-up and a beautiful amazing butterfly will emerge. But we don't see rogue caterpillars running away from the inevitability of becoming a pupa. Maybe because no one ever told it to be anything other than what it was created to be. Or maybe it's because the consciousness of a caterpillar/butterfly was not endowed with free will like us humans. Whatever it is, we can learn from the caterpillar and embrace our time as goop.

I was a bit stubborn, so it took 50 days, three deaths, and three surgeries to break me down into goop, softening my heart to allow my transformation to begin. I write this book from the perspective of goop as my transformation is still in progress, but I have a better understanding of which lessons and experiences play a part in my healing. I applied my integrated knowledge to create a framework to help guide myself and others on the journey through transformation. To be clear, true change and healing is not a passive or intellectual endeavor, it is work, and there is no way to get around that. It is also continuous as we uncover and face more of our pain and find more of our truth. I pray that readers of this book make the necessary changes in their consciousness without enduring the physical experiences I did.

Sometimes a health crisis will just happen, and we recover physically and move on with our lives doing nothing different, thinking nothing different, and feeling nothing different. The totality of what I experienced will not allow that for me. I could no longer allow "Fat, Black, and Unlovable" to find refuge within me. All the nurses and doctors that took care of me or helped to save my life; all the friends and family that visited or called regularly, cooked for my family, and supported my healing; all the prayers and positive thoughts; all the care, concern, and commitment from my husband and children — all of this made it undeniably clear that I was loved, so how could I be Unlovable? How could I not love *myself* unconditionally? I am not unlovable. I AM love. You ARE love. We all are. It doesn't mean we don't have emotions or that people don't get angry with us or piss us off. Being Love means we can open our hearts to the spiritual essence that is bigger than all of us yet is within all of us while simultaneously connecting all of us.

People often ask me if I remember anything from my firsthand experience with death and the spirit world. I do not, at least not in the traditional sense of "remember." What I have are strong feelings. I feel like a child that got called in the house and reprimanded for not playing nicely or behaving well. I get the sense that my mother had a "bone to pick" with me. She wanted me to dissolve the shadows I inherited and created so that I may live my best life, in beauty, in power, in love. I can discern that my ancestors, led by my mother, were with me throughout my entire experience in the hospital and ensured that I returned to my body each time I left. I am sure that as much as some of the emotional pain I carried in my body was intergenerational, it was also the strength of my ancestors that enabled me to survive the physical repercussions of multiple life times of stress. I am aware that my will to live was energized and activated through my family lineages, through my Ancestral Mothers and Fathers, and all those who came before me. I had always accepted and embraced my African heritage, my "Blackness", intellectually. However, emotionally, I felt shackled by it, weighed down. It was as if being Black gave me strength because it made life more difficult, so I had to flex my "muscles" more. But I now understand being Black beyond my previous over simplified intellectual construct. I see now that being Black, being a descendant of enslaved Africans, being an heir to the wisdom and sacrifices of those that survived the cotton, sugar, rum, coffee, rice, and tobacco plantations of the Caribbean and the Americas, sharing the DNA of a genius people upon whose backs the world's economy was built, this, ALL of this IS my superpower. Being Black is my power, not because it adds weight and struggle, but because it lifts me up, builds me up, and gives me life, constantly and unconditionally.

Once I got home, it took months of recovery to clear the fog of anesthesia and morphine before I could think more clearly and start to process what had happened to me. One thing that stood out to me was how much weight I lost in the hospital, more than 30 pounds in less than two months! I must admit, I liked seeing that number on the scale; I hadn't been that weight since I was 13! But I looked and felt horrible. Earlier that year, I healthily lost weight with intention, but couldn't see it when I looked in the mirror. That was the catalyst for recognizing "Fat, Black, and Unlovable" as my prevalent ever-present belief. Once I was out of the hospital and back home starting my healing journey, I saw myself in the mirror and I did not like this thinner version of me. My skin was rough and saggy, every part of me was flat and hung lifelessly. For the first time in my entire life, I had no ass! I mean nothing, zero, zilch! When I looked at it in the mirror, it looked like two deflated balloons. I had always been strong, especially my legs, now I had no strength at all. Just showering and grooming would take hours of slow-moving progress, followed by a nap and no activity for the rest of the day. I couldn't lift any objects and could barely lift my own legs. I would estimate that nearly all of the 30 or so pounds I lost in the hospital was the result of muscle wasting. Despite being at a weight I loved seeing theoretically, I did not like this body; the way it looked or how it felt. I complained about my butt or lack thereof (remember anesthesia was still crazy making in my head), but my daughter soon put that worry in perspective saying,

"Perhaps it's time to define yourself by something other than you butt." Just like that, I was checked by my own child, much like my mama would have. Bam, my complaining evolved to jokes! I loved that my body had reserves of fat and muscle to burn for healing and survival. The joke I said to my friends is that my heart ate my ass to save my life! I also came to understand that my butt and leg strength would come back as I regained overall strength through physical therapy and Pilates. Pilates became my new love that would stay with me even after insurance cut me off from PT. Slowly, I went back to the weight I was when I entered the hospital and my butt came back to me. I love and appreciate my body more than I ever have. It not only survived, but it is thriving in ways not typical considering all the physical traumas it went through. No matter how I have neglected my body in the past, staying awake when it needed rest, feeding it junk when it needed nutrition, failing to properly hydrate it, not loving it, or appreciating it, no matter how disconnected I was from my body, it did not abandon me. It survived. My body generated energy from parts of itself not essential for survival to activate the wisdom present in each cell and re-pattern my internal systems to function. Understanding all that my body has given me, falling in love with its brilliance and intelligence, I no longer see flaws and imperfections as judged by the standards of my oppressors. I see a perfectly designed, intricate elaborate work of functional art.

It is true that everyone has their own goop journey and we need to support each other through it. I have a good friend with whom I periodically exchange goop check in texts and phone calls. We say, "How goes it in da goop?!" or respond with, "Just goopin'." Revel in your goop and take the time to acknowledge someone else's progress through it. Appreciate this time when you don't have to be a certain way or fulfill someone else's expectation of you. Let go of the former you and settle into the goop. Allow the parts of you that were never yours to fall away, freeing up your energy. Explore the you that was abandoned as a child to conform to society and please the people and institutions around you. Believe in magical things. Open your heart and let love in. Soon, like the caterpillar, "Fat, Black, and Unlovable" will cease to exist and...

will fight its way out of the goop.

Scan QRCode

Visit

BeautifulPowerfulLove.com/book

to receive exclusive content for readers of this book to help support your journey. Password provided in Chapter 4.

ACKNOWLEDGEMENTS

To my mama, **Quessie Maxine** and my daddy, **Robert Charles Williams**, for dedicating your lives to raising, protecting, and loving your children and showing us what love and commitment can look like, I will forever love, honor, and be grateful for you. Thank you for giving me life.

To my **Ancestors** who survived and thrived as well as those that sacrificed their lives, all so that we may exist, I love you. I honor you. I thank you.

To my brother **Bobby** whose time on this earth was short, we never met in the physical form, but I love you big bro and I thank you.

To my sisters, **Esther, Felecia, and Lizette**, for loving me, having my back, and all the neon headbands, I love you and thank you.

To my children, **Deja and Nazir**, for choosing me as your mother, I thank you and will always love you through time and space.

To my niece, **Kim**, and nephews **Kevin, Donnell, Cornell, and Thaddeus**, for being loving pseudo siblings for myself or my kids, I love you and thank you.

To my ex-husband, **Mitchell Pamplin**, my hero for nearly two decades now, for partnering with me on adventures in child rearing, home-building, and life learning, I love you unconditionally and I thank you.

To my cousin **Dr. Sandra Branch** for being the researcher and keeper of our maternal lineage history, I love and thank you.

To my friend, ally, fellow dancer, and event planning partner, **Vanessa**, for supporting and enhancing my vision for Beautiful. Powerful. Love. events before I even finished the book, I love you and thank you.

To our friend and brotha from anotha motha, **Awo Ifatunmibi Ogunlesi**, for your support and acknowledgement through the goop, I love and thank you.

To my ex-sister-in-law, **Shelly** for lending your presence, love, and support during my final days in the hospital and the recovery period that followed. I love you and I thank you.

To my editor, **Iya Omiyemi (Artisia Green)**, for pushing me to say more and strive for excellence, I love and thank you.

To **Baba Femi** for creating OIDSI and doing what you do, I love and thank you.

To **Iya Omilana** for introducing me to Ifa and supporting my journey, I love and thank you.

To **Dora Oliveira Newman**, my Afro-Brazilian dance teacher, and **Ifẹ̀ Iná** (FKA **Mark Lilly**, my Orisha dance teacher, for teaching me a broader view of my identity as a woman descended from enslaved Africans, I love you and I thank you.

To **Monique and Aisha**, my peeps who were the first to know I was pregnant and attended La Maze class with me, I love you and thank you.

To **Wendi, the most** real sista in corporate America who help me stay grounded and cooked for my family, I love and thank you.

To **Courtenay, Anna, Alyson,** my friends and fellow lovers of dance, for demonstrating that "white fragility" can be overcome and white women can show up as allies for Black women, I love you all and thank you.

To **Dr. David Nelson, his amazing team**, and his steady hand; to **Dr. Franz Hastrup**, his quick wit, and the **Critical Care nursing team** at Overlake Hospital, I love you all and thank you.

To the many **people** who encouraged me to keep living, keep writing, and not give up, I love and thank you.

To **you**, the reader, for picking up this book and allowing me to share my story, I love you and I thank you.

To **me**, for having the courage to put my business in the streets and the tenacity to publish this book, I love me and I am thankful to be alive.

REFERENCE LIST

Brown, Brené. 2013. "The Power of Vulnerability: Teachings on Authenticity, Connection, and Courage." Louisville: Sounds True.

Brown Givens, Sonja M., and Jennifer L. Monahan. 2005. "Priming mammies, jezebels, and other controlling images: An examination of the influence of mediated stereotypes on perceptions of an African American woman." *Media Psychology* 7, no. 1: 87-106.

Cheng, Tina L., and Elizabeth Goodman. 2015. "Race, ethnicity, and socioeconomic status in research on child health." *Pediatrics* 135, no. 1: e225-e237.

Clark, Kenneth B., and Mamie P. Clark. 1950. "Emotional factors in racial identification and preference in Negro children." *Journal of Negro Education* 19, no. 3: 341-350. http://www.jstor.org/stable/2966491.

Dattel, Gene. 2009. Cotton and Race in the Making of America: the human costs of economic power. Lanham: Rowman & Littlefield.

Davis, James Allan, and Tom William Smith. 1991. General social surveys, 1972-1991: cumulative codebook. No. 12. National Opinion Research Center (NORC).

Eltis, David. 1999. The Trans-Atlantic Slave Trade [computer File]: a Database on CD-ROM. New York: Cambridge University Press.

Farber, Mark, Thaniyyah Ahmad. "Aortic Dissection (Dissecting Aneurysm; Dissecting Hematoma)." Merck Manuals Consumer Edition. Accessed January 11, 2019. https://www.merckmanuals.com/home/heart-and-blood-vessel-disorders/aneurysms-and-aortic-dissection/aortic-dissection

Fettich, Karla C., and Eunice Y. Chen. 2012. "Coping with obesity stigma affects depressed mood in African-American and white candidates for bariatric surgery." *Obesity* 20, no. 5: 1118-1121.

Gates Jr, Henry Louis. "How many slaves landed in the US?" *The Root.* Accessed January 31, 2019. https://www.theroot.com/how-many-slaves-landed-in-the-us-1790873989

Gilliam, F. D. "The 'Welfare Queen' Experiment: How Viewers React to Images of African-American Mothers on Welfare." UCLA: Center for Communications and Community. Accessed November 27, 2017. https://escholarship.org/uc/item/17m7r1rq

Halloran, Michael J. 2019. "African American Health and Posttraumatic Slave Syndrome: A Terror Management Theory Account." *Journal of Black Studies* 50, no. 1: 45-65.

"Heart Disease in African-American Women." American Heart Association. Accessed January 11, 2018. https://www.goredforwomen.org/about-heart-disease/facts_about_heart_disease_in_women-sub-category/african-american-women/.

Juang, Derek, Alan C. Braverman, and Kim Eagle. 2008. "Aortic dissection." *Circulation* 118, no. 14: e507-e510.

Leary, Joy DeGruy, and Randall Robinson. 2005. *Post traumatic slave syndrome: America's legacy of enduring injury and healing.* Milwaukie: Uptone Press.

Lehrner, A., Yehuda, R. 2018. "Trauma across generations and paths to adaptation and resilience." *Psychological Trauma: Theory, Research, Practice, and Policy* 10, no. 1: 22-29. http://dx.doi.org/10.1037/tra0000302

Panko, Ben. "Racism harms children's health, survey finds." *Smithsonian.com.* Accessed November 27, 2017. https://www.smithsonianmag.com/science-nature/racism-harms-childrens-health-180963167/

Roger, Véronique L., Alan S. Go, Donald M. Lloyd-Jones, Emelia J. Benjamin, Jarett D. Berry, William B. Borden, Dawn M. Bravata et al. 2012. "Heart disease and stroke statistics 2012 update: a report from the American Heart Association." *Circulation*. Accessed December 31, 2018. https://www.ncbi.nlm.nih.gov/pmc/articles/PMC4440543/

Staples, Robert, and Terry Jones. 1985."Culture, ideology and black television images." *The Black Scholar* 16, no. 3: 10-20.

Staples, Robert. 1973 "Race and ideology: an essay in black sociology." *Journal of Black Studies* 3, no. 4: 395-422.

Tan, Alexis S., and Gerdean Tan. 1979. "Television use and self-esteem of blacks." *Journal of Communication* 29, no. 1: 129-135.

Wade, Roy. 2015. "Racism and Its Impact on Children's Health" Webinar October 13, 2015. https://www.aap.org/en-us/Documents/cocp_racism_child_health.pdf.

Weld, Theodore Dwight, and James Armstrong Thome. 1969. *Slavery and the Internal Slave Trade in the United States*. NY: Arno Press.

INDEX

ABOUT THE AUTHOR

Barbara C. Pamplin (Ohuninifa) is a Black woman, mother of two, trauma survivor, and intuitive healer. She is a practitioner of African Traditional Religion (ATR) which means she honors and communes with Ancestors as well as reveres and studies the wisdom of nature. Barbara has a BA and MBA from Clark Atlanta University and a successful former marketing career with global companies in technology, nonprofit, advertising, pharmaceuticals, and food industries.

Fueled by gratitude and joy for living, Barbara decided to go beyond surviving to use her experiences to create Beautiful Powerful Love as a platform to share inspiration, storytelling, and coaching. She leverages her experiences to help Black women remember how to love themselves, heal themselves, and heal the world. Barbara has a unique perspective because she survived traumatic sudden changes to her body, mind, and spirit while learning to give and receive love to both herself and others.

Barbara currently lives in Washington State with her teenage son.

Learn more about her at BarbaraPamplin.com

Thank you for allowing me to share my journey with you!

Sign-up at

BeautifulPowerfulLove.com/book

to receive exclusive content for readers to help support you on your journey.

(access code provided in Chapter 4 required at sign-up)